"Singing and Dancing Across Liberia"

"Singing and Dancing Across Liberia"

A. J. Kandakai

To order additional copies of this book, contact:
Xlibris
1-888-795-4274
www.Xlibris.com
Orders@Xlibris.com
770360

CONTENTS

INTRODUCTION

Many diverse groups can take credit in many ways for contributing immensely to the adventurous undertaking I have cheerfully branded singing and dancing across Liberia.

This book profiles fifteen songs set in the tiny West African nation of Liberia. Ingredients for the fifteen songs did not emanate from the musical settings of modern day libraries located in Monrovia, Manchester City or Mansanta in neighboring Guinea. Singing and dancing across Liberia has its origins in the mores, folkways and traditions of rural communities such as the Jundu village, Tombey, Yahde and the urban slums of Cooper farm and New Kru town.

The movers and shakers who were kind enough to volunteer the oral stories, motivations, insights and historical perspectives about the rural and urban singers, cultural performers and societal icons can be safely placed into three (3) groups: Woh-meh-nus, Meh-meh-ku-meh-nus and Po-meh-nus.

Wo-meh-nus represents the totality of the village parentage. They establish and enforce rules and guidelines governing village quarters or neighborhoods. Wo-meh-nus usually know everything about the singers, dancers and instrument players in the rural and urban communities.

Meh-meh-ku-meh-nus in short, are the custodians of community knowledge and wisdom. They are the guardians of the unwritten by-laws and ordinances which govern the behavior of inhabitants and residents of the rural communities.

Po-meh-nus: these are people with some modicum of western style education. They know the movers and shakers and opinion leaders – both local and expatriate – who shape and influence governmental policies. The access granted by these diverse groups to this author over several decades is simply invaluable.

The firsthand information voluntarily shared with this author prevented reliance on second and third hand information from music shelves in Brick and Mortar libraries located at the Victoria University of Manchester and the PEPC institute of Berlin, where the author was fortunate to pursue part of his education.

While navigating the musical shelves of the New York public library and other Julliard-like musical conservatories were extremely useful, the primary source and oral information on the morals, folkways and cultural traditions of the tribal people provided by the Wo-meh-nus, Meh-meh-ku-meh-nus and Po-meh-nus remain paramount to this research effort.

The wide range of oral information, knowledge and wisdom shared with this author served as the impetus for the lyrics composed, rearranged, standardized and profiled in this book.

The author agrees with our primary oral sources that singers and musicians usually focus on key iconic targets in furtherance of their musical careers. Prominent among these targets are: Individuals or an array of personalities, momentous events, or prescribe geographical locations. A road map chatting the course of this book is now established. We wish to now ask our global reading audience to join us and embark upon an adventurous reading journey that singing and dancing across Liberia is thrilled to offer.

PART "A"

The seven songs profiled in the part A section of the book are placed in three categories: Folksy Brand, Professional brand and Populist brand songs.

This author considers himself fortunate for the extraordinary access afforded him by individuals considered to be the wisest, most experience and imbued with wisdom by members of their rural communities. These revered personalities were categorized into three groups: The Wo-meh-nus, the Meh-meh-ku-meh-nus and the Po-meh-nus. These knowledgeable elders are the primary source for the compilation of stories which are conveyed in the fifteen songs profiled in our book "Singing and dancing across Liberia". None of the stories about the songs is written down except for the song "Manja-mu-balo" the rest are oral tales about the singers and musicians and the personalities they immortalized in their songs.

CHAPTER 1

Folksy Brand songs

There are two songs categorized as Folksy brand songs in this chapter. The songs are: Beg Kegn and Gbun-Del-Ma.

Musicians identified as folksy singers have traditionally been people with little or no formal education. These singers are generally known as ordinary folks engaged in farming, hunting, fishing and other mundane task. They hum and sing songs to help them to get through their activities of daily living.

The Wo-meh-nus, Men-meh-ku-meh-nus and Po-meh-nus cautioned this author to take note of the fact that a folksy singer may be seen putting a fence made of chopped wood around his rice farm. The rice farmer may place one or more trap doors at strategic sections of the wood fencing.

The Wo-meh-nus, Men-meh-ku-meh-nus and Po-meh-nus took pains to stress that a typical rice farmer needed the blessings of the local Zoe who heads the sande or girls bush school and her cohort the Dahzoe who heads the poro or the boys bush school to perform certain ritualistic ceremonies at the beginning of each rice planting season for each individual farm.

The provisions for the typical ritualistic ceremony includes a white rooster, hardened rice pudding, red and white kola nuts, beads, twinkles and a small amount of money. After slating the throat of the rooster, the blood is spilled across the harden rice pudding.

The Zoe and the Dazoe proceed to engage in a high pitch chanting, humming and singing as they implored the souls of the departed spiritual

1

leaders to watch over this rice farm. Tradition maintain that paying homage to the departed souls will drive away the ferocious weeds, torrential rain which induce flooding as well as keeping away the rice eating birds, ground hogs, squirrels and other predators bend on destroying the farmer's rice and other food crops. Corroboration for this oral narrative can be found in our reference notes section.

A typical singing farmer can also be seen standing on a wooden platform with a sling containing pebbles designed to drive away marauding flocks of birds notorious for eating rice almost ready for harvesting.

The dipping sun with its beautiful red glow setting across the meadows, streams, valleys and rolling hills in the far western distance signals to the singing farmer that his typical working day has ended. It should be noted that the singing farmer lacks a Rolex, Omega and Apple 10 risk watches. If he had these watches he wouldn't even know how to operate these modern devices. He must therefore rely only on his body clock to warn him that his working day is fast coming to an end.

The fact that the singing farmers Jundu village has no electricity can't be denied. The village has no pipe-borne water. The medical and educational services are sub-standard. The motor road into the village is muddy and difficult to traverse for half of the year. It is also a known fact that farmer and singer Kai-Kai and his wife Hawa Jer-jeh have toiled in the burning sun, tropical rain storm, malaria borne mosquito and other biting insects throughout the year as they tended to their rice farm. Now the rice is ripe and ready for harvesting. Rice harvesting and the annual festival celebrations are on hand. The frogs are croaking, the birds are singing and happy days are here again.

The singing farmer attired in his traditional korto-kundu, standing beside his wife Hawa Jer-jeh attired in her traditional gbateh kundu garb, with young son Zukeh Bandoh, daughter Tata Mahee and hunting Dog Subah including visiting student Baka-Jani with his writing pads and many pencils departs their farming kitchen and other domestic animals for their home village of Jundu.

Beg Kegn

The folksy brand song Beg-kegn hummed by folksy singer such as farmer Kai-kai and its English translation are presented at the end of this story.

After a warm bath, family dinner and other social needs are attended to, the singer famer and his young bride both of whom are under age 25 get in touch with friends and relatives for some evening merry making.

As the full glow of the glittering moon brightens the vibrant village, young couples, old timers, singles, revelers and musicians are geared up for fun time in the village. Momo the samba or drum beating man, Bindu the sah-sah musician and Vanii the horn blower accompanied by their musical troop have assembled in the center of the village. In keeping with traditional cultural norms, a horizontal line of nine fun loving merry makers is formed behind the musicians. A second line of six follows the first line. A third line of four is formed followed by the other members of the frolicking merry makers pressed closely against one another.

These fun-loving celebrants between ages 16 and early 60s will sing and dance all night long. Corroboration for this oral narrative can be found in our reference notes section.

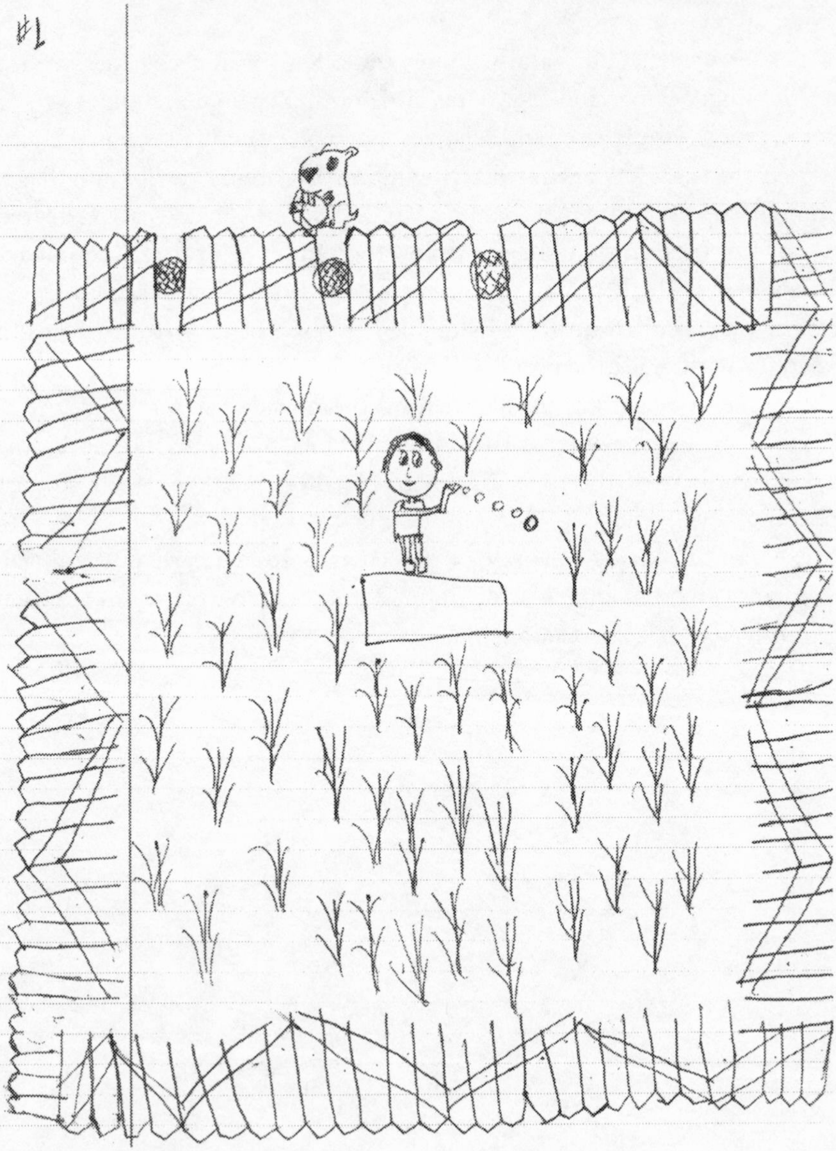
#1

Begn Kegn

Begn-kegn......koh bieh-loh 3x

Music 3x

Begn-kegn...ay ay ayay ay ay....
Begn kegn......keh messeh moh – mu 3x

Music 3x

Beg kegn ay ay ay
Begn kegn ......koto kun...du mu 3x

Music 3x

Begn kegn ay ay ay
Begn-kegn - gbeh teh kun du mu 3x

Music 3x

Begn kegn ay ay ay
Begn kegn gee bieh loh 3x

Music

Begn kegn ay ay ay
Begn kegn koo bieh – loh 3x

Music 3x   .

Beg kegn ay ay ay
Begn kegn wo – ya moh – mu 3x

Music x3

Begn kegn ay ay ay
Begn kegn Musu kay moh – mu 3x

Music 3x

Begn kegn ay ay ay
Begn kegn du yan moh – mu 3x

Music 3x

R e p e a t

Musu kay moh mu….duyan moh mu

Beg Kegn (Pants leg)
Summarized English Translation

The different stanzas in Beg Kegn will be group as A, B, C. The song Beg Kegn contains an array of personalities and stuff.

A. Beg Kegn has hydro seed (henia): Repeat 3X
Beg Kegn contains skinny legs: Repeat 3X
Beg Kegn contains male shorts: Repeat 3X

CHORUS
Lets dance my people. Repeat 6X

B. Beg Kegn contains female shorts: Repeat 3X
Beg Kegn contains water bag: Repeat 3X
Beg Kegn contains big bones: Repeat 3X

CHORUS
Lets dance my people. Repeat 6X

C. Beg Kegn hypes gossipers. Repeat 3X
Beg Kegn hypes womanizers. Repeat 3X
Beg Kegn includes everybody. Repeat 3X

CHORUS
Lets dance my people. Repeat 6X

Gbun-Del-Ma

The second song under Folksy brand is Gbun-Del-Ma. The Wo-meh-nus, Meh-meh-ku-meh-nus and Po-meh-nus were very eager to share their feelings and perspective on the song Gbun-Del-Ma. According to them the song "Gbun-Del-Ma" profiles an unforgettable character residing in a typical rural village. Gbun-Del-Ma may be described as a form of sexual harassment. Individuals engaged in this type of behavior are usually middle-aged men between ages 30-45. These individuals are usually unmarried and childless. They don't own rice farms or a cash crops farm such as coffee, cocoa or oil palm. They do not own a home in the village.

They are basically homeless, jobless and regarded as transients. Many regard them as unstable with some serious mental challenges. They will perform odd jobs for a meal and a place to lay their heads. They are usually made fun of and regarded as the butt of village jokes.

They are the ones usually cowering in corners watching young maiden as they pound the rice in the mortar with a pestle for the evening meal. This synchronizing rice cleaning procedure can be found at the end of this story. This oral narrative has affirmation in our reference note section.

While disposing of the depleted rice hubs, a maiden is sometimes grabbed and taken by someone engaged in Gbun-Del-Ma behavior. Rumors has it that they are tolerated only because they our connected to one of the well-known village families.

Gbun-Del-ma

(1) Gbun-del-ma

kai-jai-moh mu

gbun del ma

kai kpah-m0h mu

gbun del ma

bu-bah-kai mu

gbun del ma

chorus

toh bai-bai-mu

gbun del ma

toh bai-bai-mu

gbun del ma

toi-bai-bai-mu

gbun-del-ma

m u s i c

(2) musu-kay moh mu

gbun del ma

wasu kay moh mu

gbun del ma

la tai-kay moh mu

gbun del ma

chorus

m u s i c

(3) ah bunea-kay

gbun del ma

ah bunea karn

gbun del ma

ah bunea-nuh

gbun del ma

c h o r u s

m u s i c

(4) kpeh me moh mu

gbun del ma

jamba me   moh mu

gbun del ma

ta wa-me moh mu

gbun del ma

c h o r u s

m u s i c

(5) mui la suhn kay

gbun del ma

mui la sah keh

gbun del ma

mui gbeh ma jeh

gbun del ma

c h o r u s

m u s i c

13

Gbun – Del – Ma (Lover boy)
Summarized English Translation

1. He's fair skinned
   He's skinny
   He's got fat belly

   CHORUS
   He's a lover boy
   He's nothing but trouble:
   Repeat 3X

2. He's a womanizer
   He's full of cheek
   He's a confusionist

   CHORUS
   He's a lover boy
   He's nothing but trouble:
   Repeat 3X

3. He calls the young maiden
   He steals the young maidens
   He hides the young maidens

   CHORUS
   He's a lover boy
   He's nothing but trouble:
   Repeat 3X

4. He's a drunk
   He loves weed
   He likes tobacco

   CHORUS
   He's a lover boy
   He's nothing but trouble:
   Repeat 3X

5. Let's convene the meeting
    Let's do the feast
    Not everyone is here

    CHORUS
    He's a lover boy
    He's nothing but trouble:
    Repeat 3X

CHAPTER 2

The Professional Brand Songs

➤ Qui-Lay-Mu-Lai
➤ Jeh-Mu-Bah
➤ Vai Rap

The second chapter in singing and dancing across Liberia profiles the professional brand songs. These are songs composed by professionally trained musicians. The audience includes the educated class such as doctors, lawyers, engineers, teachers, politicians and the ruling classes of civil society.

The three songs which exemplifies the professional brand category are Qui-lay-mu-la, Jeh mu-bah and Vai rap.

Following a series of lengthy discussions amongst themselves the Woi-meh-nus, Meh-meh-ku-meh-nus as well as some Po-meh-nus arrived at the consensus viewpoint about the characters immortalized by the professional brand singers and musicians. The wo-meh-nus and Meh-meh-ku-meh-nus asserted that the professional brand singers many times idolized both iconic and villainous characters in their songs. The song Qui-lay-mu-lai vividly portrays such an opinionated and villainous character. They informed this author that the character memorialized in Qui-lay-mu-lai; the first of the professional brand songs is presented as the scion of a mythical kingdom. The leader of this legendary kingdom is king Leopard. The isolated island kingdom is alleged to be surrounded by a body of salt water. It is this kingdom that boy Leopard claimed to be his home. Upon arrival at Yahde village, Boy Leopard a muscular teenager who is approximately 6 ft. tall and weighs about 250 lbs. He arrives on a Suzuki motor bike as the sun set on the western edge of the Yahde village.

The teenager headed directly to the chief's compound upon arrival at the Yahde village. He introduced himself as Boy Leopard, son of King Leopard, ruler of the Island kingdom. The chief ordered one of his wives to provide the youth with food and overnight accommodations.

At dawn, Boy Leopard visits the chief and tells the chief and his assembled elders of the many adventures he experienced since he left his father's island kingdom. He inquired if there is a resting place for birds near the village. The chief summoned two of his teenage sons and other nephews and asked them to accompany Boy Leopard to the nearest bird sanctuary. As they approached the sanctuary, a flock of pigeons took off from the nearby tree. Boy Leopard leapt into the air and grab one of the biggest pigeons in the flock.

The accompanying young followers burst into laughter while cheering his ability to capture a flying bird. The party returned to the chief's compound with the prized pigeon. The pigeon is dressed and roasted over embers of charcoal. The pigeon is chopped up and the town chief is given the breast and the neck of the pigeon. Boy Leopard is given the pigeon's thigh and the wing. To the utter surprise of the assembled elders and chief, Boy Leopard demands that he be served the breast and neck of the pigeon. One of the elders calmly explained to Boy Leopard that all necks of chicken, ducks, pigeons, geese and other flying birds can only be consumed by the town chief. At this juncture Boy Leopard claimed that he had been abused and disrespected by the chief and his elders and did not want to listen to any more of the stupid customs and traditions of the chief and his elders.

He abruptly storms out of the meeting and heads towards his Suzuki bike. Feeling belittled and insulted by the hot-headed youth, the chief rose from his chair coughed loudly and sent a cursed-filled spit towards the rear of the angry young man. Unperturbed boy Leopard hurried towards his Suzuki bike loudly singing the lyric qui-lay mu la oh. He leapt on the back of his Suzuki bike and rolls out into the rising morning sun light. Blinded by the rays of the rising sun boy Leopard took a steep bend in the road with the Suzuki bike accelerating to its top-notch speed causing the angry young man to lose control of the powerful Suzuki bike. The Suzuki bike crashed into the rear of a poorly-parked lumber truck instantly killing boy Leopard.

The Wo-meh-nus and the Meh-meh-ku-meh-nus orally passed on this story as an example of what befalls opinionated characters with very little social skills.

Another message the Wo-meh-nus and the Meh-meh-ku-meh-nus wanted conveyed is that tempestuous behavior may lead to self-inflated tragedy similar to the one that befell Boy Leopard following his unfortunate interaction with the chief and elders. The opinionated youth's visit with the skull in one of the stories told in "The Land of the Pepper Bird" by author De La Rue illuminates the wisdom of the gray beards. This oral narrative has affirmation in our reference note section.

The literary meaning of the lyric of the song is "I am the son of king Leopard, take me back to my father's kingdom". The song "qui-lay-mu-la" can be found at the end of this story. The summarized English translation of this song can also be found at the end of this story.

CHORUS

Qui lay mu la ho..............

qui lay   mu-la ho-yo..

woh tan-da man jah   bah

1.

de ya de-dea...ho-yo

woh tan da man jah bah

mano de dea, ho yo

woh   tan   da man jah bah

wee-doh de-dea..ho yo.

woh tan-da man jah   bah

c h o r u s

2

dambla de dea ho yo

woh tanda man jah bah

tei ne de dea ho yo

woh tanda man jah ma..

mambo de dea ho yo

woh tan-da man jah bah

c h o r u s

3

Bendu de dea h0 yo

1

woh tanda   man jah bah

jundu de dea ho yo

woh tanda man jah bah

voin-zuan de dea ho yo

woh   tan-da man jah bah

c h o r u s

4

Tombay de dea ho yo

woh tanda man jah bah.

Garwular de dea ho yo

woh tanda   man jah bah

5

Taiwoh de dea ho yo

woh tanda man jah bah

wahkor   de dea ho yo

woh tanda man jah bah

chorus

2

Qui – Lay – Mu - La (Songs/daughters of the King)
Summarized English Translation

CHORUS
We are children of the King
We are children of the King oh yes
Please take us to the King

1. Deya biter oh no
   Take us to the King
   Mando biter oh no
   Take us to the King
   Weedoh biter oh no
   Take us to the King

CHORUS
We are children of the King
We are children of the King oh yes
Please take us to the King

2. Dambla biter oh no
   Take us to the King
   Teine biter oh no
   Take us to the King
   Mambo biter oh no
   Take us to the King

CHORUS
We are children of the King
We are children of the King oh yes
Please take us to the King

3. Bendu biter oh no
    Take us to the King
    Jundu biter oh no
    Take us to the King
    Voin-zuan biter oh no
    Take us to the King

    CHORUS
    We are children of the King
    We are children of the King oh yes
    Please take us to the King

4. Tombay biter oh no
    Take us to the King
    Talla biter oh no
    Take us to the King
    Wahkor biter oh no
    Take us to the King

    CHORUS
    We are children of the King
    We are children of the King oh yes
    Please take us to the King

5. Taiwoh biter oh no
    Take us to the King
    Garwular biter oh no
    Take us to the King
    Kpopa biter oh no
    Take us to the King

    CHORUS
    We are children of the King\
    We are children of the King oh yes
    Please take us to the King

Jeh-Mu-Bah

Jeh-Mu-Bah, the second song in our professional category chronicles the exploits of several larger than life Vai traditional cultural characters.

These iconic personalities can be divided into (3) groups. They are the teaching character, the writer character and social commentators.

The teaching characters engaged in research activities high lighting the role of Vai musicians, entertainers and story tellers in the rural communities of the Vai country side. Popular musicians such as Sekou Gbondeh entertained folks attending events such as marriages and religious ceremonies.

The writer characters memorializing songs like "Jeh mu bah" are numerous. These are the writers who specialized in popularizing the Vai script. They have argued that the Vai script is unique.

The Wo-meh-nus, Meh-meh-ku-meh-nus and Po-meh-nus have once again assembled at elder Zukeh Kandadai's quarters in the Jundu village. The attraction to elder Zukeh's quarter of the village was obvious. For some time now, he has served as the Dean Elder of the Kiazolu clan. The holder of this position was not compensated financially. The Dean Elder title was simply honorific. It was however common knowledge that if the Dean Elder had persuasive skills he could greatly influence the role of the Kiazolu clan in the culture and the politics of Grand Cape Mount county.

It is generally accepted that the Wo-meh-nus, Meh-meh-ku-meh-nus and the Po-meh-nus were advanced in age. Most of the Wo-meh-nus and Meh-meh-ku-meh-nus were retirees. They no longer ran their rice farms and cash crops such as coffee, cocoa, piassava and oil palm.

Many of them felt obligated to visit the home of the Dean Elder and help him entertain guests and visitors arriving from all parts of the county. Many visitors regarded the Dean Elder as the repository of knowledge who had a unique perspective of both local and national politics. There were times when the dean elder hosted British colonial administrative officers from the neighboring British Territory of Sierra Leone. The elderly retirees even alleged that some visitors came from faraway places such as Guinea. The Wo-meh-nus, Meh-meh-ku-meh-nus and some Po-meh-nus boasted of rubbing shoulder with European and American visitors including young Peace Corp volunteers assigned to schools across Grand Cape Mount County.

Free food and beverages were part of the Dean Elder lagest that attracted an array of visitors. According to insider information shared with this author, a typical Dean Elder daily menu would appear as follows:

The dean elder breakfast:

Key elements of the breakfast include: boiled cassava, eddoes, sweet potatoes, plantain and roasted cassava.

A typical breakfast plater would include small portion of bust butter or blue brand margarine spread over the cassava and other tubers on the plate. A small portion of omelet or scramble egg. A slice of butter pear (avocado) and a slice of paw-paw (papaya) enhance the breakfast platter. A small coffee mug with a tea spoon of Maxwell, a cube of St. Louis sugar or a small drop of molasses and a cup of water was also served. Lastly, a medium tumbler (cup) of pine wine could be served with the breakfast platter depending upon the availability of the cherished brewed or affodicia.

Dean Elder Lunch:

The most popular Dean Elder lunches served would be a dish of Cassava Leaf with ingredients such as: chicken, dried fish, meat, crab and shrimp. The lunch must contain a bowl of king rice – the Liberian staple food. Another dish would be a bowl of check rice (green rice) accompanied by a bowl of palm oil soup (too-jai-kpondoh) – which would contain ingredients as those in the cassava leaf dish. Thinly sliced cucumber when available along with thinly sliced pineapple usually served as accompanied dessert.

Dean Elder Diner:

Dean Elder diner plater included a smaller portion of rice, fried fish or fried chicken. A few pieces of fried plantain are added when available. Drinking water was always available.

Post Diner Snacks:

A few members of the Dean Elder entourage maybe served post diner snacks. This exclusive group are usually considered the most knowledgeable, experience and influential cohost of the Dean Elder. These cherished members were usually served a few Jacob's crackers and tiny slices of cheese with a small cup of Ovaltine or related night time beverages.

It is against this background that the Wo-meh-nus, Meh-meh-ku-meh-nus and Po-meh-nus decided to address matters involving the invention of the Vai script by Dwalu Bukelleh as well as the songs and music immortalizing this momentous cultural event.

Notwithstanding their preferences for professional independence, most Vai literary icons agree about their love and respect for one larger than life cultural character. His name is Dwalu Bukelleh.

Let us start by putting the Dwalu Bukelleh's story in context. The Wo-meh-nus, Meh-meh-ku-meh-nus and the Po-meh-nus argued that Dwalu Bukelleh is regarded as a literary giant and the inventor of the Vai script. To appreciate the importance of Bukelleh's invention readers must first appreciate the role of written language and communication in the rise and spread of global civilization.

Englishmen invented the English alphabet. The Arabs, Japanese, Chinese and others invented their respective alphabets. The alphabets were essential in the development of words in the languages enumerated above.

Once formed, words evolved into sentences. Sentences were then used to communicate messages. These steps led to the development of universal education and mass communication.

The Wo-meh-nus, Meh-meh-ku-meh-nus and the Po-meh-nus cautioned this author that there were some descension in their ranks concerning a uniformed position on how the Vai script was invented. In-order to satisfy the divergent view points on the matter they urged this author to present two versions of how the script was invented. The first version is the traditional and luck-based position. This traditional pathway was supported by many of the Wo-meh-nus, Meh-meh-ku-meh-nus and the Po-meh-nus. It is also the position supported by many rank and file Vais, American and European scholars including academicians at the University of Hamburg, Germany.

The traditional and luck-based story that Dwalu Bukelleh had a dream in which he was given the Vai script is corroborated in several western publications. This oral narrative has affirmation in our reference note section.

The Wo-meh-nus, Meh-meh-ku-meh-nus and the Po-meh-nus proceeded to urge this author to present an alternative reward-base version of the Dwalu Bukelleh vai script invention story.

Events surrounding this alternative reward-based version now follows. Dwalu Bukelleh's role in the development and spread of the written word cannot be told until he crossed path with the pine wine thief. For most rural dwellers such as Dwalu Bukelleh, a pine wine tree was a prized possession. Bukelleh and other dwellers from their rural village of Bandakoh visited their pine trees during the evening hour to prepare the cones at the top of the pine tree to produce the cherished pine wine by the early hours of the next morning.

Bukelleh's palm tree was regarded as the largest and most productive of all the palm trees located near the edge of lake Piso; the largest salt water lake in western Liberia.

As the rainy season began to turn into the dry season, Dwalu Bukelleh observed that something strange was happening to his palm wine production.

Many mornings after climbing to the top of his pine tree, he observed that his cone contain no pine wine. While his larger tree produced no wine, his friends reported that their smaller trees continue to produce pine wine: that intoxicating beverage admired by most male village dwellers.

As a curious villager Dwalu Bukelleh was determined to solve the mystery of the missing palm wine episode. He decided that he would camp out in the bushes adjacent to his palm tree for a couple of nights.

Nothing happened during the first two nights of camping out at the pine wine site. Bukelleh decided the third day would be his last night camping out at the site of the palm tree. As early dawn approached on the third day and as Bukelleh struggled to keep his eyes open, there was a large splash from the edge of Lake Piso. Emerging from the lake appeared a crocodile like creature, resplendent in an outer garment of silver and black color. The creature quickly scrambled to the bottom of the palm tree and discarded his outer garment. The creature proceeded to climb using all force of his leg to the top of the pine tree. This scene of the creature climbing the palm tree is illustrated at the end of this story.

Starring with wild eyes in utter amazement with some trepidation, Bukelleh regained his composure and got into motion. He emerged from his hiding place, dash to the foot of his palm tree, grabbed hold of the creature's abandoned silver and black garment and took off running as fast as he could toward his Bandakoh village.

He did not stop to catch his breath until he arrived at the village wooded cemetery. He carefully folded the outer garment and hid it underneath some palm branches. He hastily ran through the village to the house of village chief Mambu. He whispered in the chief's ear that he had just witnessed a dramatic incident.

He asked chief Mambu to accompany him back to the village cemetery. After viewing the creature's garment, the chief instructed Bukelleh to return to the town and fetch a large empty rice bag and take it back to the cemetery. Village chief Mambu and Bukelleh proceeded to put the creature's garment into the empty rice bag and transfer the bag back to the residence of the village chief.

Village chief Mambu, a wise man and cunning leader was convinced that the garment owner would make an attempt to get in contact with dwellers of the village near the palm wine tree he had raided. In the early evening hours of that remarkable day, chief Mambu posted six of the bravest young men from the village at the out sketch of the village.

They were instructed to pay attention to any intruder coming from Lake Piso. They were further instructed that any intruder from the lake should be immediately reported to him.

Having installed the security perimeters around his village, chief Mambu proceeded to send his wife and children away from his residence. Chief Mambu turned to Dwalu Bukelleh and told him that he would be spending the night with him at his residence. Bukelleh agreed to spend the night with the chief.

Just after midnight, chief Mambu and Dwalu Bukelleh were awaken by a knock on the front door. The chief opened his front door and was astonished to find the crocodile – like creature standing at his door step surrounded by the six brave young men. Chief Mambu, Dwalu Bukelleh and the six young men were taken by complete surprise as the crocodile-like creature announced in a halting voice that his name was Baka-Fondo. The creature proceeded to claimed that he was the son of the underwater king known as king Baka.

The creature asked for a private audience with chief Mambu and the individual who has taken custody of the outer garment. Chief Mambu graciously agreed to Baka-Fondo's request. The chief invited Baka-Fondo and Dwalu Bukelleh into his private quarters and asked how he could be of assistance to his invited guest.

The creature who had introduced himself as Baka-Fondo explained to the chief and Bukelleh that pine wine was a highly cherished drink in his fathers under water kingdom. He further explained that his father, king Baka was in poor health and that he the son was expected to succeed his father upon his death. Baka Fondo told the chief and Dwalu Bukelleh that the last request his father had made of him was to provide him with one large jug of pine wine to be served at his last official feast prior to his death.

The creature Baka-Fondo expressed his apology and appeared remorseful for stealing Dwalu Bukelleh's pine wine during the many months he had raided the Bandakor village dweller's pine tree. He promised that there will be no further raiding of Dwalu Bukelleh's palm tree. He then proceeded to ask town chief Mambu to use his good offices in getting Dwalu Bukelleh to return his outer garment. The creature explained that he could not return to the underwater world without his outer garment. The chief and Bukelleh entered an adjoining room for consultation. The chief convinced Dwalu Bukelleh that they should return the creature's outer garment conditioned on some form of reward from the underwater family.

Baka Fondo, the son of the underwater king agreed to the reciprocal arrangement. He declared to chief Mambu and Bukelleh that three days after his return home he will appear in the form of a dream as Bukelleh slept. He declared that the reward will not be pecuniary but will only be knowledge. Agreeing to the compact, chief Mambu and Bukelleh return the outer garment to Bako-Fondo. Chief Mambu then instructed the six brave young men to escort Baka-Fondo to the edge of lake Piso with a large jug of palm wine.

Just around midnight, after the third day of creature Bako-Fondo's return to his underwater kingdom Dwalu Bukelleh experience a dramatic visitation as he slumbered in dream land. A gray bearded crocodile like creature sitting on the golden throne called out "Bukelleh, Bukelleh, Bukelleh" You are awarded these alphabets. Proceed to utilize these alphabets to develop a written language for the benefit of your people and human kind.

An illustration of the clay tablet with a message written in the Vai script is found at the end of this story.

When Bukelleh awoke from his sleep, he found a clay tablet next to him with the strange alphabet emblazed on the front surface ushering in the birth of the Vai script.

Songs like Jeh-mu bah tells the stories and sings praises of both heroic and vallineous characters. The song Jeh-mu bah embellishes the cultural and societal achievements of not only Vai script inventor Dwalu Bukelleh but also those of his many admirers such as Former Liberian counsel general to Hamburg Germany Momolu Massaquoi, Tombay Kai Dempster, Zukeh Kandakai, Jangaba Johnson, C. Kei Kandakai, Bai T. Moore, and other high achievers including the Wo-meh-nus, Meh-meh-ku-meh-nus and the Po-meh-nus.

Zukeh Kandakai, one of these high achievers was encouraged by some German anthropologists and linguists to work with them on the development of the Vai script at the university of Hamburg, Germany in the early 1950s.

The first dream of Bukelleh admirers was quite simple. The dream that the settler dominated political and bureaucratic elites would set aside their well-known prejudices against their fellow indigenous Liberian compatriots and accord recognition to Bukelleh's intellectual achievement.

The admirers dreamed that educational policies would be established to utilize the Vai script in developing curriculum to teach Liberian youth language arts, math and the sciences to advance the socioeconomic development of Liberia.

It is sad to report that up to the time of this publication this dream has not materialized.

Undaunted the admirers had a second dream. Since the English alphabet and those of the Arabs, Japanese and Chinese are recognized and celebrated by European and American linguists and anthropologists the admirers were of the opinion that the same recognition would be accorded Dwalu Bukelleh's Vai script.

The admirers argued that the script is not influence by any English language phonetics. The script is unique as those of the English, Arabic, Japanese, and Chinese alphabets. The only difference between those alphabets and Bukelleh's Vai script is that the Vai inventor is a village dweller from the rural village of Bandakoh located in the tiny west African nation of Liberia.

Without any research funding from philanthropic institutions such as Ford Rockefeller, Carnegie & Pew – who usually boast of providing research funding to promote literacy, protect endangered languages and preserved historical landmarks – is a further justification as to why their second dream remains unfulfilled.

During my research for this book, I was surprised to hear of a third major dream. Nurtured by Bukelleh's admirers – including the Wo-meh-nus, Meh-meh-ku-meh-nus, and the Po-meh-nus a universal concern is the apparent lack of interest by UNESCO in events surrounding the Vai script.

While the yeoman-like work of UNESCO in war torn country like Iraq, Syria, and other hot spots is highly admired, its role in the Vai script debate leaves much to be desired.

Our readers will no doubt want to see UNESCO take an active role in the preservation of the Vai script. Such steps will encourage education, social cohesion and national harmony. It will also promote religious tolerance, peace and national reconciliation among the tribal groups of the country.

Until the Liberian authorities and friends of the Vai script can get UNESCO moving, this is another dream hanging in limbo. While the key dream of most of Dwalu Bukelleh's admirer remain largely unfulfilled, the Jeh-Mu-Bah beat goes on.

The song Jeh-Mu-Bah appears in its entirety at the end of this story. Jeh–Mu–Bah (Come back to us) and yes, readers, there is a cd out there for you singers, dancers and music lovers across the globe.

#7

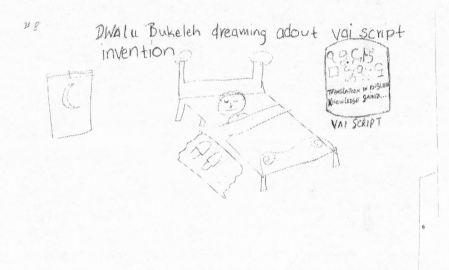

Dwalu Bukeleh dreaming about vai script invention

VAI SCRIPT

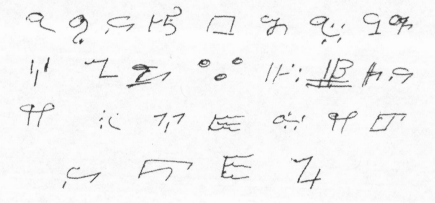

**THE KNOWLEDGE GAINED BY DWALU BUKEL FROM THE VAI
SCRIPT IN JONDU, SHOULDN'T BE ALLOW TO GO IN VAIN.**

JEH MU BAH

Sekou gbon-del

Lun boh moi

chorus

ma da sekou

jeh mu bah

2 Bah doh-doh

Kun soh moi mu

chorus

ma da doh-doh

jeh mu bah

3.Zukeh Bandoh

Kpo Giah moi

chorus

ma da Zukeh

jeh mu bah

chorus

Musa Ben

Dah-zoe moi

c h o r u s

ma da musa

jeh mu bah

5.Kai Kwe Fe-weh

men zah-moi

marda fe-weh

1

Jeh mu ba

chorus

6 kai kwe Tombay .

Kpo yean   moi

chorus

Ma Da Tombay

Jeh Mu   Bah

7 Coneh -Sheriff

Mui mua nu

chorus

Con-neh sheriff

Jeh   mu bah

8 Kai Kwe -Fahn buah

Kun Kpeh-moi

chorus

ma da   Fahn buah

Jeh mu bah

9. Vani Mar bu

man ja mui

chorus

man ja mar-bu

Jeh mu bah

teacher Kortu

mui teacher

2

teacher Kortu

jeh mu bah

Dwalo   Bukelleh

Kpo yean mui

Dwalo Bukelleh

jeh mu bah

3

Jeh – Mu – Bah (Come back to us)
Summarized English Translation

CHORUS
Come back to us. Repeat 3X
1. Sekou Gbondua
   Come back to us
   Grandpa Sekou
   Come back to us

CHORUS: 3X

2. Baido Doh
   Come back to us
   Grandpa Do Doh
   Come back to us

CHORUS: 3X

3. Zukeh Bandoh
   Come back to us
   Grandpa Bandoh
   Come back to us

CHORUS: 3X

4. Musa Ben ben
   Come back to us
   Grandpa Musa
   Come back to us

CHORUS: 3X

5. Kai Feweh
   Come back to us
   Grandpa Feweh
   Come back to us

CHORUS: 3X

6. Kai Tombey Kai
    Come back to us
    Grandpa Tombey Kai
    Come back to us

CHORUS: 3X

7. Kai Fahnbua
    Come back to us
    Grandpa Fahnbua
    Come back to us

CHORUS: 3X

8. Corneh Sheriff
    Come back to us
    Grandpa Sheriff
    Come back to us

CHORUS: 3X

9. Varney Marbu
    Come back to us
    Grandpa Marbu
    Come back to us

REPEAT 3X
    Come back to us
    Y'all thank you
    Come back to us
    Y'all thank you
    Come back to us
    Y'all thank you

Vai Rap

Vai rap, the last song in the professional category of songs in this chapter vividly illustrates humor, ridicule and satire regarding many songs in our popular culture.

The singer starts his music by mockingly bad-mouthing the lack of safe drinking water, affordable electricity, adequate roads as well as medical and related services. The singing sage proceed to shout at the top of his voice that schools and jobs are woefully lacking. This sentiment is corroborated in Daily Observer's Keith N.A. Best's book "The Other Side of Roots". This oral narrative has affirmation in our reference note section. He goes on to rally his compatriots to return to their home villages and towns in-order to correct the inadequacy of the ruling classes.

Vai rap like other humorous and satirical songs captures the spirit of another contemporary Liberian singer named Luckay Buckay and his group whose rap song laments "If they don't hit a dog my pot can't boil". So So good friends, check out "Vai rap" which comes at the end of this story.

VAI RAP

Kia Bay So Bai- Bai

Kia Bay So Bai-Bai

CHORUS

Bay Meh—Keh

Mua Manja

Toi Meh Keh

Mua Manja

Mu Kun Soh

Mu Sah-Boh

Mua Manja

2. Lampo Bay

Gee Bay Neah

CHORUS

3.Boi Bay *neah*

Kia Bah Bah → Toi bah bah

CHORUS

4,Kah –Keh Bah *neah*

Kundoh Bahn

Chorus

5th. Soi Keh- Bay *neah*

Jah—Oh Bai Bai

Soi Keh Bay *neah*

Vai Rap
Summarized English Translation

The song Vai Rap portrays the singers critical comments on the state of socio- economic developments in his/her homeland.

1. The roads are full of potholes.
   The bridges are falling apart

   CHORUS
   What's up our chief
   There's trouble our chief
   Let's consult/discuss with our chief
   Let's do a sacrifice our chief

2. There's no electricity
   There's no water

   CHORUS
   What's up our chief
   There's trouble our chief
   Let's consult/discuss with our chief
   Let's do a sacrifice our chief

3. Medication is lacking
   There's no leisure

   CHORUS
   What's up our chief
   There's trouble our chief
   Let's consult/discuss with our chief
   Let's make a sacrifice our chief

4. Schools are poor
   Food is lacking

   CHORUS
   What's up our chief
   It's trouble our chief
   Let's consult/discuss with our chief
   Let's make a sacrifice our chief

5. There's no job
   Is all poverty

   CHORUS
   What's up our chief
   It's trouble our chief
   Let's consult/discuss with our chief
   Let's make a sacrifice our chief

6. Let's return home
   Let us all return home

   CHORUS
   What's up our chief
   It's trouble our chief
   Let's consult/discuss with our chief
   Let's make a sacrifice our chief

CHAPTER 3

The populist Brand Songs are:

➤ Manja-Mu-Balo
➤ Ha Keh To

"Manja-Mu-Balo"

For many musicians, the populists brand category of songs profiles the lives of individuals, groups, momentous events as well as their geographical surroundings. The Wo-meh-nus, Meh-meh-ku-meh-nus and the Po-meh-nus appeared to have a collective sense of emotional attachment to this category of songs and the musicians who immortalized them. The Wo-meh-nus and their cohorts proudly reminded this author that their Dean Elder Zukeh was personally involved in developing the lyrics of the Manja-Mu-Balo song. They proceeded to point out to this author that elder Zukeh had acquiesce in modifying the title of the song from Kam-bai Mubalo to its present title in-order to appease a larger group of rural dwellers. The Po-meh-nus and their cohorts took pains to explain to this author that elder Zukeh's lyrics was meant as a rallying cry: a cry not to arms but to solicit self-help initiatives in the field of education, rural health services, food production, rural road building and maintenance, child care, senior care, sanitation and other community services. The lyrics were meant to mobilize a sense of self help initiatives not only across Grand Cape Mount county – across the Vai landscape of WAKOH – as well as across the length and breadth of Liberia. The Po-meh-nus exerted that the lyrics call for love, religious tolerance as well as a welcoming spirit towards all Liberians. The Po-meh-nus and their cohorts exerted that these self-help initiatives were important since more than 80% of funding for rural educational and health services were provided not by the central government but by private missionary groups mostly from the west prior to the Tubman administration. They also acknowledge that some educational services had also been provided by some Arab missionaries. The Wo-meh-nus and their cohorts appeared convinced that some of the lofty lyrics found in the Manja-Mu-Balo song were a manifestation of some of the personal disappointments and dash hopes that elder Zukeh and many like him had experience in dealing with powerful segments of the Liberian society. Many songs in this category evoke passions and emotions about past achievements as well as sacrifices of a number of musicians. The two songs memorialized in this category are: Manja-Mu-Balo and Ha-keh-to.

Many Vai traditionalist and cultural icons have long considered the song "Manja-Mu-Balo" as the potential anthem of the Vais. The original lyric to the song was taught to many students enrolled in schools such as The House of Bethany, St. John's, and other schools in Robertsport. The song was also taught to students in rural schools such as Mboloma, Jundu, Bendu, Deyah, Mambo, Dambala, Baindaja, Bomboja and other rural villages.

As time have changed due to the 14 years of civil war and other tragedies across Liberia, teaching the lyrics of this song to young scholars have become the exception rather than the norm across Grand Cape Mount county.

This is why it becomes a sad spectacle that only the elderly and the few resourceful young Vai men and women are able to participate in the singing of this celebrated song considered by many as their traditional anthem at funerals and other public events amongst the Vai populist.

Our readers shall no doubt be pleased to avail themselves of the celebrated traditional potential Vai anthem, "Manja-Mu-Balo", presented at the end of this story.

MANJA - MU - BA - LO

ma-ja mu ba lo

1. ma ja mu ba lo

mu fal-lui kpeh

mu yon   nu   leah

ai je   neh kwah

c h o r u s

ke mu jo loh foh

mu wei yeh nah

yah man   jah-jah balo

2. Du-yan meh loh

yah tan   noi koloh

mui   saa ba-boh

mui gbe ai kwa

c h o r u s

ke mu jo loh foh

mu wei ye nah

yah man   jah jah balo

3 mui to-may feleh

mui meh zai zai

mui yah soi keh

wah koh ai-kwah

c h o r u s

ke   mu jo loh foh

mu wei yeh nah

1

yah man jah jah balo

4. mui mei sah-sah

mui sah bai-boh

mui yah-soi-keh

wah-koh ai   kwah

c h o r u s

ke mu jo loh foh

mu wei yeh nah

yah man jah jah balo

2

Manja – Mu – Balo (Great chief bless us all)
Summarized English Translation

1. Great chief bless us all
    Make our hearts clean
    To love each other
    In your kingdom

    CHORUS
    Let's never forget
    How great thy kingdom is

2. In this great world
    Your praise is high
    Let's make the big sacrifice
    For all of us

    CHORUS
    Let's never forget
    How great thy kingdom is

3. Let's follow the stars
    Let's make bold statements
    Let's do the work
    For Wakor (Cape Mount) sake

    CHORUS
    Let's never forget
    How great thy kingdom is

4. Let's make bold statements
    Let's make the big sacrifice
    For all of us
    Let's do the work
    For Wakor (Cape Mount) sake

    SPEECH:
    Let's clean our hearts

Let's love one another
Let's make bold statements
Let's do the work for Wakor sake
Let us all make the sacrifice for Liberia
Thank you all, thank you all
Good bye to all, good bye to all

CHORUS
Let's never forget
How great thy kingdom is

5. Great chief bless us all
Make our hearts clean
To love each other
In your kingdom

CHORUS: Repeat 3X
Let's never forget
How great thy kingdom is

"Ha-Keh-To"

The song "Ha-keh-to" is the last song in our populists' brand category of songs profiled in the part "A" section of our book: Singing and Dancing Across Liberia.

The folksy category of songs was meant to provide entertainment for the uneducated and unsophisticated folks as they go about their activities of daily living. The song "Jeh-Mu-Bah" and similar songs in the professional category embellishes the achievement of icons such as Dwalu Bukelleh. "Manja-Mu-Balo" and "Ha-keh-to" exemplified the populists brand category of songs.

The song "Manja-Mu-Balo" evokes a sense of nostalgia for the glorious days of the past while highlighting our frailties and acknowledging our short comings. The song "Ha-keh-to" also portends an optimistic future for the lovers of music and merry making.

As we conclude the profiling of our part 'A" songs and move to our part "B" songs, we are pleased to present the song 'Ha-keh-to" at the end of this story.

Ha keh to

1

mu ma kiah-sah

na mui nu

mu ma ke-en soh

na mui nu

mu ma sign sah –

na   mui nu

chorus

woh ha keh toh   ma ma nu x 2   each

woh ha keh toh pa pa nu

woh ha keh toh na mui nu

woh ha keh toh duyan-gbe   Everybody

② music

mu wa su kay – Cheeky

na mui nu

mu la tai kay   Fuzzy

na mui nu

mu tin keh kay   Fight

na mui nu

chorus

music

3

mu fo h boh — Lazy

na mui nu

mu kah kah — konky

na mui nu

mu kun kpe h — hard head

na mui nu

chorus,

music

4

mu ma vah soh x2

na mui nu

mu fa ni — lie

na mui nu

mu musu kay — woman loppa

na mui nu

chorus

music

Ha-Keh-To (We Are Sorry)
Summarized English Version

The song Ha-Keh-To means we are sorry. This song is a listing of a number of things and behaviors people in the community failed to do for which they are expressing their sorrow and apology.

1. We didn't build the roads: Repeat 2X
   We didn't build the house: Repeat 2 X
   We didn't build the bridge: Repeat 2X

   CHORUS
   We are sorry Mamas: Repeat 2X
   We are sorry Pappas: Repeat 2X
   We are sorry People: Repeat 2X
   We are sorry Neighbors: Repeat 2X

2. We are cheeky: Repeat 2X
   We are trouble makers: Repeat 2X
   We like picking fights: Repeat 2X

   CHORUS
   We are sorry Mamas: Repeat 2X
   We are sorry Pappas: Repeat 2X
   We are sorry People: Repeat 2X
   We are sorry Neighbors: Repeat 2X

3. We are lazy: Repeat 2X
   We are rascals: Repeat 2X
   We are stubborn: Repeat 2X

   CHORUS
   We are sorry Mamas: Repeat 2X
   We are sorry Pappas: Repeat 2X
   We are sorry People. Repeat 2X
   We are sorry Neighbors. Repeat 2X

4. We didn't build the village: Repeat 2X
   We told lies: Repeat 2X
   We are womanizers: Repeat 2X

CHORUS
We are sorry Mamas: Repeat 2X
We are sorry Pappas: Repeat 2X
We are sorry People: Repeat 2X
We are sorry Neighbors: Repeat 2X

LONG RYTHM

Part "B"

The eight English language songs profiled in the part "B" section of this book are group in two categories:

Traditional & Nostalgic as well as Contemporary & Transitional brand songs. The traditional & nostalgic brand songs are: Happy Birthday Sufferman, Eternal Chief, Take Me to The King, Happy New Year. The Contemporary and Transitional brand songs are: Only He Can Fix it, We are Buddies, Working People Rapping and Happy Birthday.

CHAPTER 1

The traditional & nostalgic brand songs

"Happy Birthday Sufferman"

The Po-meh-nus and their cohosts were very forceful in helping this author understand the importance of the folk ways, mores and traditions of the society out of which these songs have their origins. Many songs are written to sing praises to the powerful and the lionized. Yes, musicians usually strive to separate the beautiful, the handsome and the celebrated from the lowly and the down trodden. And yes, while many others cruised by in their BMW's to shopping centers of their choice, many in the happy birthday sufferman song communities must make do with coupons at the Aldi's and Dollar Generals to feed their families. While others enjoy ivy league legacy educational opportunities, the suffermen types of their communities are left with no options but to strive to gain access to crowded community colleges.

And yes, many of those in the well-off communities will agree that tackling the challenges of feeding families, trying to gain access to affordable education and entry in the job market leaves little or no time for recognizing and honoring special days in the suffer man community.

It is for these and other reasons that the well off in society must start to recognize the need to honor the special days of our less fortunate members of our communities. We can do this by rising and joyously singing not in cacophony but perfect harmony: happy birthday to you suffer man.

The text for this song recognizing the plight of those celebrated by the song 'Happy birthday sufferman" can be found at the end of this story.

HAPPY BIRTHDAY SufFeRMaN

Suffer man

Streets are mean

Towns are bad

CHORUS

Happy birthday to you suffer man

MUSIC

2. Fares are high

Food is scare

CHORUS

Happy birthday to you srffer man

MUSIC

3. Back to school

Done with school

CHORUS

Happy birthday to you   suffer man

MUSIC

4. Get a job

Settle down

CHORUS

Happy birthday to you suffer man

MUSIC

5. Rock and roll

Time to dance

1

CHORUS

Happy birthday to you suffer man

MUSIC

6. Gone with strive

time to sing

CHORUS

Happy birthday to you suffer man

MUSIC

2

"Eternal Chief"

There are multitudes of reasons given for the composition of the original lyrics of the song "Manja-Mu-Balo" – whose literary translation is great chief bless us all. Eternal chief is the English version of the song "Manja-Mu-Balo" whose original lyrics were introduced by elder Zukeh Kandakai of the village of Jundu.

My grand papa Zukeh admitted to me at an early age that his primary reason for composing the song "Manja-Mu-Balo" was to protest the practice of indenture servitude. Indenture servitude was the practice of holding men, women and children in bondage against their will.

Elder Zukeh took pains to explain to me that he Zukeh was the grandson of the warlord Fahn Manu. Fahn Manu was also the patroit of the house of Jundu. The name of Jundu is a corruption of the name Junloo which means the nest for slaves in the Vai dialect. It is against this horrific background that Eternal Chief, the English version of elder Zukeh's manja-mu-balo is written.

Acknowledging past transgressions, the lyric in the first stanza of Eternal Chief begs for the cleansing of our hearts so that our love is shared with those we may have transgressed against.

Lyrics in subsequent stanzas recount the vastness of the universe and promotes the sharing of bread amongst our common humanity. In taking these steps, the Vais can put their shoulders to the wheel and work for peace and social cohesion in Grand Cape Mount county and across the length and breathe of Liberia.

Our version of elder Zukeh's original song is intended to compliment the goal and aspirations Dean Elder Zukeh presented in such an eloquent manner in his pioneering song.

My version of Eternal Chief would not have been possible without the foundation laid in the elegant words of "Manja-Mu-Balo". All credit for both songs goes to Dean Elder Zukeh of the village of Jundu.

Our readers and music lovers can find the full text of the "Eternal Chief song at the end of this story.

Eternal Chief

1. Eternal Chief do cleanse our heart, to share our love in fellowship

CHORUS

To pledge to all in all places, how great thou power is

M-U-S-I-C.

2 In this vast world your praise is high

You stage the feast for us to eat

CHORUS

to pledge to all in all places, how great thou power is

MUSIC

3.We see the stars in yonder sky, we do the work for wah-koh sake

CHORUS

To pledge to all in all places, how great thou power is

MUSIC

4 We know the laws protect us all, we do the work for wah-koh sake

CHORUS

To pledge to all in all places, how great thou power is

1

"Take Me To The King"

The third song in the traditional and nostalgic category in the part "B" section of this book is entitled "Take me to the king". The primary message conveyed by the song "Take me to the king" revolves around value laden attributes such as dishonesty, deceit and fraudulent behavior.

The roles those character traits played in the composition of the song "Take me to the king" cannot be fully appreciated until we have identified the village dwellers whose lives are impacted by songs such as "Take me to the king".

It all started with the dawn of the dry season. This is the time when the rice crop on the various farms were ripe and ready for harvesting. It was also the time when the bush school for the young girls have ended. The bush school – referred to as the sande bush for girls – is a traditional institution for providing skills to enable young girls to become functioning wives and future mothers in the rural communities. This was the period when the sande bush conducted its closing ceremony. The confluence of these activities left the Yahde village in a joyous and festive mood.

The author was reminded by the Wo-meh-nus, Meh-meh-ku-meh-nus, Po-meh-nus and their cohorts that the community structure of the Yahde village is comprised of three groups: The town chief and his council of elders, Zoe Began (head mistress of the Sandi institution known as bush schools for girls) and her cohort Da–Zoe Boima-head master for the poro institution (known as the bush school for boys) and members of the general community.

As expected, the village chief and his council of elders ran the affairs of the Yahde village. Zoe Began and her cohort Da-zoe Boima assisted the village chief and his council of elders in assuring that the young adult woman and men were adequately trained and properly supervised.

The rest of the citizenry and residents of the village comply with the rules and regulations set by the village chief and enforced by Zoe Began and her cohort Da-zoe Boima.

It was Friday evening, the first day of the rice harvest festival: an occasion eagerly anticipated by the village folks of the Yahde village. As the sun began to set on the far western horizon, farmers from various farms began to stream into their beloved Yahde village. Each family of man, woman and children headed to their individual quarters. Everyone took their evening bath, changed into their evening garments and congregated into their social groupings. As the children horse play around, the men told stories, while joking, laughing and enjoying each other's company.

The women whose work never seem to end started the preparation of the evening meal. As large pots of newly harvested rice were being cooked, the accompany pot of veggie such as cassava leaf, potato green, pallava sauce and other cherished veggies were being prepared to be cooked.

Vai cooking culture allows for chicken, beef, and fish to be lumped together with the veggies in one pot. When onions and other condiments are in place, a measure helping of palm oil is added and spiced by queen pepper. The combined aroma of newly harvested rice, a mouthwatering pot of veggie readily permeates each quarter of a ready to eat Yahde village.

While waiting eagerly to be called to partake in their evening dinner, a strange group of travelers arrived at the center of Yahde village. It was a middle age couple with a ten year old child, who claimed to be a travelling sooth sayer healing family. They asked to be taken to the village chief's compound.

Upon arrival at village chief Dodoh's compound, they informed the chief that they had travelled from a northern kingdom beyond the Guinea highlands ruled by king Madodo. They explained to village chief Dodoh that they were professional sooth sayers (card readers) and healers.

All struck by this revelation, chief Dodoh dispatched a messenger to fetch Zoe Began, head of the sandi bush for girls. The zoes responsibilities included mid-wifery, FGM rituals, cuts, contutions, broken limbs and other abnormalities. Zoe Began was the acknowledged medicine woman of the Yahde village.

Da-zoe Boima, head of the poro bush for boys was the chief's principal assistant and zoe Began's professional cohort. He too was summoned to the chief's compound. By the time zoe Began and da-zoe Boima responded to the chief's summons, most of the town folks had already formed a circle around the chief's palava hut.

Chief Dodoh proceeded to inform his people that the travelling sooth sayers and healers had made an important prophecy about their village. The essence of the prophecy was that their village was sitting on top of a vast quantity of gold and diamond.

He told the town people that the sooth sayer and healing family would show them the entrance to the gold and diamond treasure if the town people agree to provide a small gift package to the sooth sayer and healing family for the benefit of the ancient prophets.

Many of the town folks began to wonder about the nature of this gift package. The answer to the question was fast in coming. Each family head is required to bring back to this palaver hut in the next one hour the most precious piece of jewelry that is most dear to your hearts. Now go back to your homes, gather that piece of jewelry and bring it back to this palaver hut as quickly as possible. The village people quickly dispersed in obedience to the chief's instructions. The visiting family were passed onto da-zoe Boima to provide them food and overnight accommodations.

As soon as the palaver hut and its surroundings were cleared of the village people, zoe Began, the head medicine woman of the town and her cohort da-zoe Boima sprang into action. They both remembered a similar visitation by people resembling this family of sooth sayer and healer some 8-10 years back. That was during the reign of village chief Dodoh's late father. The prophecy during that visitation was that the creek running next to the Yahde village was full of gold, diamond and other precious metals. Regrettably that visiting family never return to the Yahde village to substantiate their prophecy. Concerned that visitors claiming to be sooth sayers and healers could undermined their authority, they asked for a private audience with village chief Dodoh.

They expressed their concern to the chief and argue that these visitors appeared to be dishonest, deceitful and fraudulent in their presentation.

The chief asked them for a plan to deal with the situation. Zoe Began – the high priestess magician and leader of women had a ready plan. The plan had two phases:

The first phase of zoe Began's plan was to open the side of a pillow and place bed bugs at strategic locations inside the pillowcase which was to be placed on the bed assigned to Saidu, son of the sooth sayer and healing family.

Zoe Began's calculation was that immediately after midnight the bed bugs would start crawling out of the pillow and periodically start to bite the neck, facial area and arms of the young boy throughout the rest of the night. The biting bed bugs traumatized young Saidu to the point where he was banging on his parents' bedroom door at the first crack of dawn. Young Saidu told his parents that he had been bitten by bed bugs throughout the night and pleaded with them to call upon the chief-or king as they refer to village chief Dodoh – to provide them their reward, relief and goodies and send them on their way back home.

The second phase of Zoe Began's plan called for placing a small cobra in a calabash container. When the last family head had brought their precious jewelry, all of them should be sent back to their respective homes.

The chief zoe Began and da-zoe Boima would then retire to a secluded location. The plan called for a piece of precious jewelry to be placed inside the small calabash container. Zoe Began offered to place one of her small cobras in the middle of the calabash containing a piece of precious jewelry enclosed in the jar with its lid shut tightly. When dawn broke, the chief, the visitors and everyone else were done with their breakfast, the visitors and the town folks were summoned to the chief's palaver hut.

The chief proceeded to present the gift package to the sooth sayers and healing family. The sooth sayers and healers thanked the village chief and his people for their hospitality and the gift package presented to them. They promised to take the gift package to a holy site where they will conduct a special presentation to the ancient prophets. They promised to return to the Yahde village and escort the chief and his people to the entrance to the mine containing the gold and diamond treasure. This announcement brought great joy to the people; leading to hugging, hands shaking and back slapping.

It was at this juncture that chief Dodoh bid the travelling sooth sayer and healing family farewell and save travelling. He told the departing travelers of one specific request. He told them to stop walking after 30 minutes from the Yahde village. Right after they stop walking, the jar containing the precious jewelry should have its lid remove and their young son Saidu should place his hand inside the jar and feel for something similar to a heart shaped object. The object would be part of a piece of jewelry placed in the jar. After grabbing that object, the boy should then remove his hand from the jar containing the precious jewelry.

According to zoe Began's plan young Saidu's finger would be bitten before he could extract his hand from the calabash jar containing the precious jewelry and this is exactly what happened to young Saidu. Following the bite of the cobra Saidu fell to the ground and began foaming at the mouth. Panic-strickened, the family recalled village chief Dodoh's instruction to return to Yahde village if anything should happen to them during the course of their travel.

The panic-stricken family hurried back to the Yahde village with their convulsing son. Village chief Dodoh, zoe Began, da zoe Boima, the elders and some prominent town folks were still loitering around the palaver hut.

Zoe Began and her cohort da zoe Boima were not surprised to see the visiting family return to their village in a panicking mood. Village chief Dodoh demanded to know why the family had returned to the Yahde village. The family explained that they believe a cobra had bitten their son.

The body language of the parents revealed to village chief Dodoh that this couple were not prophets and healers as they had alleged. He decided to go for the juggler. If you admit to me, in the presence of these witnesses that you are no prophets and healers, I will arrange to help save the life of your son. Realizing that their cover had been blown, young Saidu's father and mother knelt before chief Dodoh and in a quivering voice admitted that they were part of a gang of scammers who had a misguided view of the inhabitants of the forested region of the continent. They regarded the rural dwellers as an intellectually unsophisticated, gullible buffoons ready to be taken for a ride.

Realizing time to save the boy's life was quickly slipping by, chief Dodoh instructed zoe Began to use her magical power to save the boy's life. Zoe Began did not hesitate. She opened a small calabash basket sitting next to her and retrieved a small bottle filled with herbal syrup. She took a sip from the bottle, goggle it in her mouth and spat it out. She then took the index finger of young Saidu which was infected with the venom of the cobra. She placed the finger in her mouth and sucked out the bloody contents and spat it out. She took a second sip of the herbal syrup and goggle it in mouth and spat it out on the boy's finger. She then opened a small can containing an ointment like cream and rubbed the cream on young Saidu's finger. Mesmerized, chief Dodoh and the assembled crowd remain silent. In less than 15 minutes, little Saidu sat up and asked for a drink of water. He then asked for some food.

After eating a bowl of rice cereal, young Saidu began jumping up and down in a state of joyful ecstasy. His parents thanked and bear-hugged chief Dodoh and zoe Began and thank her profusely for saving their son's life.

After eating a big bowl of rice and a healthy serving of cassava leaf, chief Dodoh asked his town people to show mercy and compassion on the dishonest, deceitful and fraudulent couple. He returned the donated jewelries to each of the families.

As a sign of personal compassion and forgiveness, the chief took his gold-plated watch with its dangling charms and draped the watch around the neck of the ten-year-old Saidu. Chief Dodoh told the assembled crowd that he had an emotional bond to the watch. He explained to the crowd that they were aware that he and his wife had no children. He informed the group that the watch had been sent to him by an American peace corp volunteer that he and his wife had adapted when the volunteer served as a school teacher in the village some years back. They had named the volunteer Bindu-Vana.

The chief told the group that his adopted daughter, Bindu-Vana would replace the gold-plated watch after he had appraised his adopted daughter about what had happened in the town in the past 48 hours.

The chief's wife and prominent women of the town put together a food package and presented it to young Saidu's mother. After admonishing the couple never to return to his village, chief Dodoh bid them farewell and send them back to their northern kingdom.

It is events such as the visit of the prophetic and healing family along with anecdotes from the Wo-meh-nus, Meh-meh-ku-meh-nus and Po-meh-nus and their cohorts that led this author to compose the song "Take me to the king". Our readers can find the full text of the song "Take me to the king" at the end of this story.

Take me to the King

Tarwo De Dee bites all night long
Mama papa what can I do
Take   me to the King for   my rewards
Take me to the King for my relief
Take me to the king for my goodies

Hun-hun-hun-hun-hun

Garwular De Dee bites all night long
Mama papa what can I do now
Take me to the King for my rewards
Take me to the king for my relief
Take me to the King for my goodies

Hun-hun-hun-hun-hun-hun

Tobay De De bites all night long
Mama papa what can I do now
Take me to the King for my reward
Take me to the king for my relief
Take me to the King for my goodies

Hun-hun-hun-hun-hun

Wah kor De De bites all night long
Mama papa   what can I do now
Take me to the King for my reward
Take me to the King for my   relief
Take me to the King   for my goodies

Hun-hun-hun-hun-hun

"Happy New Year We Are Still here"

The last song in our traditional and nostalgic category is entitled "Happy New Year We Are Still Here". The original source of this song emanates from oral stories shared with this author from our Wo-meh-nus, Meh-meh-ku-meh-nus, Po-meh-nus and their cohorts regarding a song which can only be described as the potential Kru anthem commonly known as "Happy new year me no die-yo". The literary translation means happy new year I did not die. I survived to see the new year. This author's research about this traditional and nostalgic song dear to the hearts of Kru musicians spans a quarter century of listening to oral stories narrated by our Wo-meh-nus and their cohorts coupled with similar stories shared by our Kru brethren reminiscing about their folk lore and stories about the horrific Sasstown war. The Wo-meh-nus, Men-meh-ku-meh-nus and Po-meh-nus took pains to explain to this author that even though anthropologically different from the Mende-Tan and Mende-Fu groupings the Krus who inhabited a large chunk of the eastern, central and costal portions of the country has always been held in high esteem by the Vais for their bravery and enterprising spirit. This view of the strategic territorial location of the Krus in Liberia is corroborated in our reference note section.

Both the Wo-meh-nus and Kru oral story tellers reminded this author that following the Sasstown crisis, many young Kru men travelled abroad as itinerant immigrant workers. They travelled to overseas communities working in deplorable conditions in places such as Freetown, Accra, Lagos, Boston, New York city, Blackpool, Liverpool as well as in tough neighborhoods in other far-flung communities across the globe.

The author is also the beneficiary of ancillary information regarding the Krus. These includes food preparation, family life, dress code and fashion. Other taste includes the love for jewelry, hard work, leisure and having a jolly good time. These and other tribal information were generously shared with this author by many Kru elders including Mama Mary Chea and other friends and acquaintances and my deceased aunt Justine Nimely and Momolu Kandakai.

My research collaborators were generous in providing me an insightful view of the typical Kru personality. Refusing to be absorbed into the Liberian body politic, the Kru warrior chieftain Nimely launched a secessionist conflict historically known as the Sasstown war.

The Liberian authorities mobilized their forces and defeated Nimely and his compatriots in a decisive battle in Sasstown. The krus quickly put Nimely and the civil conflict behind them and embraced their Liberian citizenship.

When the ensuing new year arrived, former Kru combatants – men, women and children – gathered around lunch tables graced with palm butter dishes. The palm butter dish must always include multiple fish, shrimps, crabs, kiss-me but never exclude king shark fish, the ingredient that is the ultimate spice for a typical palm butter dish. For the combatants and others that survived the Sasstown war and were able to see the new year gladly rejoice as they hear the melodious tune of the song "Happy New Year Me-No-Die-Yo".

Following the Sasstown civil conflict, many Krus embraced Roman catholic and other educational opportunities, specializing in areas such as nursing, sanitation and other community services. Other interest included vocations such as book-keeping and accounting services, teaching, apprenticeship in law and politics. Some activist Kru politicians included D. Tweh, Tuan Wreh and Tippoteh.

Irrespective of all their achievements, nothing excites a typical Kru community-Be it Old Kru town, Clara town, New Kru town, Colonel West and similar communities – than the arrival of a visiting Kru male or female from the many overseas communities they inhabited.

They dress in apparel smacks of the latest fashion. Their jewelry and blin blin demonstrated what evolves on the streets of Lagos, Liverpool, New York city and New Orleans.

When the newly arrived binto kru psychedelic step on the dance floor in Nagbe bar in New Kru town, other dancers quickly clear the floor. This was the time to show all and sunda the new salsa, rumba, cha-cha, jitter bug, the electric slide, twist and other favorite gigs.

Many of these cultural movers and shakers arrived during the week and days approaching the new year season. They usually brought gifts of suits and dresses for their parents as well as designer sun glasses and tops for their kids, nephews, nieces, and other relatives.

Many had toiled in factories and assembly line to sacrifice some money for the big trips back home to celebrate the coming new year. Many may have missed many funerals of their departed love ones. When the show-man shift on the dance floor was over, the binto usually hurry home to sleep before the dawn of the happy new year morning. Many Revelers arrived with empty bottles, empty metal pots and other abandoned utensils, as well as drum and sticks which targeted the residency of the binto. The singing in unison of the familiar song of "happy new year me no die yo" awaken the typical binto.

For many of them this was the first time they heard the familiar song in one year, five years, ten years or more years. The song brought back fond memories of departed family members while reassuring others of how lucky they were to be alive to celebrate the new year. The song "Happy new year me no die" was conforming, refreshing, somber yet exhilarating.

After the early morning breakfast, the customary palm butter dishes began arriving from all parts of the community. The bintoes took great joy in dressing in their outfit carrying the labels of max and spencer found in Liverpool department stores as well as Tommy Hilfiger found in Fifth avenue department stores in New York city. The women having prepared their palm butter dishes, local pastry doughnuts, rice bread-are dressed up in elaborate lace embroidery kentay garments. They have visited the hair saloon and their manicures and pedicures have been taken care of. The blin blin is there for us to behold. Some of the binto men are dressed in pink strips suits, a waist coat and dangling gold watches.

As clusters of families and friends enjoy their shark sweetened palm butter dishes, the kids are running around with bottles of Fanta, coke and Kool-Aid. The new year celebrants are not only enjoying themselves, they are also imbibing in servings of aromatic schnapps, Heineken, Guinness, club beer and other adult beverages. Yes, in Sasstown, Picnicess, Grand cess, New Kru town and other Kru communities across Liberia and the world wild kru diaspora.

The new year is being celebrated and "happy new year me no die yo" is loudly proclaimed by all red blooded Kru families.

It is against this traditional and nostalgic perspective that this author was inspired to compose the song "Happy new year we are still here".

Our readers will find the full text of the song "happy new year we are still here" at the end of this story.

HAPPY NEW

We are still here, great joy

Special greetings to you all...we love you

REPEAT

A

Mama Sara

Mama Naomi

Mama Marte

Mama Hetty

Mama Alice

Mama Siatta

Mama Justine

Mama Gina

Mama Sadie

Mama Sando

Mama Tombay

Mama Lulu

Happy New Year we are still here, great joy

Special greetings to you all, we love you

B

Mama Jartu

Mama Massa

Mama Kemah

Mama Bindu

Mama Zina

Mam Deweh

Zoe Gambi

Mama Zoe Keiah

All The Zoes

Mama Hawah

1

Al The Hawas

Mama Tata

Mama Jane

Mama Waytay

Happy New Year we are still here, great joy.

Special greetings to you all

C

Mama Jarbo

Mama Berma

Mama Jerbo

Mama Zukeh

Haja Teh-tee

Jerbeh- Hyjay

Mama Korlu

Mama Sarda-mah

Mama Ora

Mama Emma

Mama Gbowolo

Mama Darbo

Mama Mai ma

Happy New Year we are still here, great joy.

Special greetings to you all

REPEAT

2

CHAPTER 2

Contemporary and transitional songs

The contemporary and transitional section profiles four songs. These are: Only He Can Fix It, We Are Buddies, Working People Rapping and Happy Birthday

"Only He Can Fix It"

The four songs in this section generally highlights the socio-economic challenges faced by inhabitants of our urban centers.

The Wo-meh-nus, Mem-meh-ku-meh-nus, Po-meh-nus and their cohorts are once again prominent in narrating our oral stories about the singers and musicians who have immortalized the characters profiled by the songs in this category of the book.

The economic communities in these urban neighborhoods were uneven. The urban metropolis of Monrovia hosted over four hundred thousand inhabitants in the early 1960s. There was only one YMCA available to provide leisure services for the urban youth. There were no city parks, there were no public pools, there were no neighborhood soccer fields. Soccer after all is the national past time.

With these leisure services woefully absent, elders, families and young adults usually congregate under shaded plum trees indulging in games such as ludo, snake and ladder, checkers, scrabble and various card games to accommodate their leisure needs.

The Po-meh-nus and their cohorts warned this author that social services could not be provided to the rural and urban communities because of the poor management of Liberia's scarce resources. This criticism of the inaptitude by the Liberian political classes to manage the country's fiscal resources is corroborated in our reference note section.

It was in these social settings that the story about successful and failed marriages were discussed. The adults discussed the status of the political deliberations occurring across the country. The role of education in the socio-economic development of the country was a favorite topic for discussion. A career in which one work for the government or pursued a career in the private sector engender passionate debates.

Many of the elders and individuals representing many career paths distinguish themselves during these lively discussions. One of the most articulate and popular participant in these checkers board card playing debates was a middle age eight grade graduate popularly known as Mangold.

Unlike his younger brother who had completed the 12th grade with a wife who held a nursing aide certificate both of whom served as employees of the national government Mangold vocally and loudly proclaimed that he was an entrepreneur who worked in the private sector. While his brother and sister in-law work from pay check to pay check, sometimes waiting for ninety days to get a pay check Mongo, a hands-on gold and diamond miner claimed to always have access to ready cash. A stark example of Mangold's financial success was a ten-bed room dual purpose residence he erected without a bank loan.

When Mangold-whose front teeth were encased in gold casings check out in a matching bracelet and gold blin-blin spoke-youngsters looked at him in awe and wonder and believe every word he uttered.

It was in such a setting and at such a time that Mangold took the liberty of sharing many stories with his adoring audience. Of the many stories Mangold told, one had an impactful significance for this author. This was the story about the life, the successes and the dramatic ending of the legacy of the character Mongo called Boer-man. Our readers are now invited to hop aboard and suck-in the story of the Boerman family odyssey.

Boerman was born in a gold mining family somewhere in southern Africa. Following the independence movement of the early 1960's, his family's gold mining business was nationalized. Unable to find suitable employment, young Boerman embarked upon a sea faring career.

With the rudimentary mechanical and electrical skills he had acquired while working in his father's gold mining business, young Boerman obtain employment as an electrical technician aboard an ocean-going cargo vessel.

The vessel picks up goods from the west African ports of Lagos, Accra, Conakry, Monrovia and Dakar trading them with imported goods from the ports of Liverpool, Breman and Hamburg. The vessel MV Bismarck called at the port of Monrovia at 90-day intervals. While discharging cargos from vessels like the MB Bismarck, many of the vessels younger crew members enjoyed their leisure evening hours at bars and entertainment centers strunk across the boulevard from the Freeport of Monrovia.

Being a free spirit, Boerman asked a local taxi driver to take him to a low-class neighborhood further down the boulevard from the port. The taxi driver took Boerman to a rockers neighborhood joint called Nagbe bar. Boerman entered the facility and observed that all the seats were taken. He felt like a minority since he was the only one of a different race among the patrons of the bar. As a celebrated patron, Mangold was sitting on the bar stool right across from the cashier of the bar. Only high rollers occupy the bar stools at the Nagbe bar.

Boerman ordered a sixteen-ounce becks and stood against the wall sipping his refreshing brew. Next to Mangold was a bar stool occupy only by his personal pouch. Mangold gazed across the bar and observed a lonely looking European guy sipping from a sixteen-ounce becks bottle. Mangold pointed at the guy and yell above the music and said, hey dude, come up here and have a seat. Mangold removed his pouch and Boerman hop upon the stool. The effervescent Mangold introduced himself and proceeded to ask his seat mate about his name and his reason for visiting Nagbe bar. Both guys appeared to have similar personalities and took no time to become fast friends. After a couple of rounds of drinks paid for by Mangold, the pair exited the bar together. Using his taxi cab as his personal transport during his leisure time, Mangold offered to drive Boerman back to the gate of the Freeport. Mangold and Boerman exchanged telephone numbers and Boerman went through the gates of the port and headed to his vessel while Mangold headed home.

It was a little after three months and Boerman was on the phone telling Mangold in an excited voice that his vessel had just birth at the wharf of the Freeport of Monrovia. It was after midday on a balmy Saturday afternoon. Boerman informed Mangold that he would be done with his task aboard the vessel by 5pm. Mangold responded that he would pick up Boerman at about 6pm for an early dinner at his residence. During the evening Mangold introduced Boerman to one of his neighborhood friends. During dinner, Boerman and the pretty lady known as Mama Lulu appear to share an endearing chemistry.

As the dinner ended, Boerman asked Mangold if he could invite Mama Lulu to accompany them on their planned evening visit to Nagbe bar. Mangold responded positively and invited his female friend to make the bar visit a foursome. They had drinks at the bar and dance until the wee hours of the morning. By the time they departed Nagbe bar, Boerman and Mama Lulu were romantically joined at the hips.

By early Monday morning Boerman was back on his vessel as it sailed north bound for its European port of Blackpool. While Boerman was in Europe, Mangold return to his gold and diamond mining operation in Wasua tucked in the forest of western Liberia.

Early one afternoon, Mangold was called to the radio in the mining office. Mama Lulu was on the radio and could not contain her excitement. She told Mangold that Boerman had called her early that morning and ask her to marry him. She also told Mangold that she had agree to the marriage proposal.

When Boerman's vessel return to the Freeport of Monrovia and disembarked from the vessel loaded with their wedding outfits, a present for Mangold and many gifts for Mama Lulu and her teenage son fondly called Flambo.

Boerman and Mama Lulu's wedding was an entertaining and enjoyable neighborhood event. Boerman rented a two-bedroom apartment and settled in with his newly formed family. Following his honeymoon, Boerman and his friend Mangold sat down over becks and had a heart to heart talk about going into a mining partnership. They leased a failing gold and diamond mine and turn the operation into a profitable venture in less than five years. Using his southern African connection Boerman became the gold and diamond buying agent for the DeBeers Mining conglomerate with offices in Antwerp, London and Midtown Manhattan in New York city.

In less than ten years Boerman had built a four-bed room house in the exclusive Mamba Point neighborhood of Monrovia.

Their son Flambo now in his early 20s had expressed the desire to become an actor. Boerman and his wife Mama Lulu always eager to indulge their son in all kinds of kakamina ideas, dispatched him to Los Angeles to pursue his acting career in Hollywood.

By the fifteenth year of his gold mining venture, Boerman had become the richest gold and diamond mining agent in the country. He had built a couple of rental apartments and dominated the gas station business across the country. Boerman had also taken up piloting small planes as a hobby. Meanwhile the DeBeers business partners kept pushing Boerman to come up with a certain brand called blue diamond. Boerman continue to push Mangold and his miners to pursue the veins leading to the diamond sites.

With his newly found wife Boerman and Mama Lulu acquired a frontline Mercedes Benz and a top of the line Cadillac STS sedan. Boerman was now financially comfortable to employ a chauffeur to transport he and his wife Mama Lulu in their comfortable Benz and Cadillac vehicles. A skillful casino black jack card player became the man everyone referred to as Boerman's creole chauffeur. On weekends when Boerman was in town from the mine, he, his wife Mama Lulu and his creole chauffeur frequently visited the casinos where they played black jack, share Havana cigars and enjoy rounds of adult beverages.

It was after one of these late-night casino outing that Boerman got a call from Mangold that he and his mining crew had hit pay dirt with the discovery of two four corner blue diamonds. Even though Boerman had been warned that a thunder storm was approaching the areas surrounding the Weasua air strips, Boerman could not wait to put his hands on those blue diamonds.

Boerman had his single engine cessna aircraft gas up and took off from the Spriggs Payne airport for the one-hour flight to Weasua. Boerman was in radio contact with the Weasua air strip control towel for most of the flight time. However, during the last fifteen minutes of his ETA at the Weasua air strip he ran into a furious thunder storm, he lost control of the aircraft crashing into a bunch of mahogany trees surrounding the airport.

A search party was organized and within 48 hours the charred body of Boerman was found in the burnt-out aircraft. As maybe expected, Mangold, his mining crew, Boerman's wife Mama Lulu and their friends were devastated by the sad news of Boerman's untimely death.

As the family prepared for Boerman's funeral, Flambo, the playboy son return home from his failed acting adventure in Hollywood.

Some six months after Boerman's tragic accidental death and funeral, his wife Mama Lulu summoned Mangold to Monrovia for a business meeting. It is now some fifty (50) years after this author and his high school friend Sackor sat listening to Mangold narrate his many stories – many of which were funny and hilarious told under the plum tree-back in 1962.

It is now 2012 and many of us from our Newport street Cooper farm days are visiting Mangold to reminisce about events from our younger days.

In discussing what Mangold described as the Boerman saga, he recalled being told by Boerman's widow Mama Lulu that she and the creole chauffeur were now a married couple. Mangold remembered Mama Lulu telling him the ceremonies were being performed by a justice of the peace and witnessed by her son Flambo. Mangold noted that neighbors told him that Mama Lulu's mother called the creole chauffeur a gambler and a smooth-talking parasite. The mother refused to attend the wedding. Listening intensely to Mangold's story and sitting at the edge of our seats, Mangold dropped the bomb shell. Mangold record Mama Lulu pointing at him and saying consider yourself fired. There is no partnership agreement between you and my late husband. You were just an employee, as an executrix of my late husband's business enterprise, I have every right to dismiss you from your post. My husband, the creole chauffeur taxi driver's brother is authorized to take over your post.

Mangold recalled that he was simply dumb founded and speechless at the turn of events between he and his good friend Mama Lulu. Mangold recalled returning to the mining operation in Weasua where he broke the news of his dismissal to his mining crew. Furious at the unfair manner in which Mangold had been treated, they decided to walk off the job. With Mama Lulu's newly minted creole chauffeur husband and playboy son, playing the absentee managers, the mining operation came to a grinding halt.

Meanwhile, creole chauffeur husband and don't carefy son Flambo were busy gambling at the various casino strips around greater Monrovia. With little or no supervision all of Boerman's businesses began tumbling downward.

As news reached Mama Lulu that the gold and diamond business had failed just as the creole chauffeur husband and good for nothing son kept betting at the casino, Mama Lulu began crying and went on lamenting and alluding to phrases such as man oh man what a mess, boy oh boy what a mess, you don't know the answer – only he – meaning her late husband Boerman – can fix it.

Unperturbed by the gold and diamond failure, the parasitic husband and son two-some convinced Mama Lulu to borrow money and invest in a ruby and silver mining venture in a neighboring country. As this business venture failed and the husband and son kept betting, Mama Lulu kept lamenting and crying, man oh man what a mess-boy oh boy what a mess-only he can fix it.

By the time the amateurish husband and son investors had traversed the bronze, bauxite, emerald and sapphire failing ventures, Mama Lulu had lost her Mamba Point residence along with her gas station and rental apartment business ventures.

Mangold in a quivering voice with tears running down his cheeks told the assembled group how he had visited Mama Lulu's bedside as she began slipping away from an overdose of sleeping tablets.

The composition of the song "Only he can fix it" is a small attempt by this song writer and author to memorialize the deeds and words of a neighborhood giant known to all of us as our beloved Mangold. We are pleased to share Mongold's grief-stricken story narrated to the assembled group. Mangold revealed how Mama Lulu held his hand tightly and whispered to him in a weak voice saying, brother Mangold, I am sorry before taking her last breath.

We are pleased to share the full text of the song "Only he can fix it" at the end of this story. Then next the English lyric of this song follows

Gold and diamond miners
Papa keeps biting
Mama keeps crying
Bankers are waiting

Chorus
Man oh man what a mess
Only He can fix it
Boy oh boy what a mess

Only He . can fix it
 You don't know the answer
Only He can fix it

Rubies and silver
Papa keeps biting
Mama keeps crying
Agents keep waiting

Chorus
Man oh man what a mess
Only He can fix it
Boy oh boy what a mess
Only He

 can fix it
You don't know the answer
Only HE can fix it

Bronze and bus ate miners
Papa keeps biting
Mama keeps crying
Debtors keep warning
Chorus

Man oh man what a mess
Only HE can fix it
Boy oh boy what a mess
Only HE can fix it
You don't know the answer
Only HE   can fix it

Emerald and sapphire
Papa keeps biting
Mama keeps crying
Vulgar keeps poking

"We Are Buddies And Trusted Friends"

Our oral story tellers, especially the Po-meh-nus and their cohorts were instrumental in sharing with this author the genesis of the story regarding the principal character whose life story motivated the composition of the song entitled "We Are Buddies", this iconic character is said to have migrated from the James town neighborhood of Accra a major West African city. Papa Kweku and nephew Tombux were a fisherman family who settled in Robertsport, the urban capital of Grand Cape Mount county. Robertsport is a cape that sits on top of a monstrous rock sandwiched between the Atlantic Ocean on the east and Lake Piso on the west.

There is consensus among geographers that the Portuguese navigator Vasco da Gama name this rock "Grand Cape Mount" because it was the largest of the six capes found around and within the African continent. The other capes were described by Vasco da Gama as Cape Montserrado, Cape Palmas, Cape Coast, Cape Verde and Cape Town. The Atlantic Ocean and Lake Piso provides a boundless reservoir of marine life for the fishing community.

Papa Kweku joined members of the fishing community in erecting his residence on the eastern slope of the city of Robertsport just above the Atlantic Ocean. His first store was in the grass field district where most of the working-class community maintained their homes and businesses.

Everyone in this working-class district knew one thing about Papa Kweku's fish store; You only got your fish if you pay the full 100% of the price charged by Papa Kweku. While Papa Kweku and his family lived in a home located in the most affluent neighborhood of the city, he had very few friends among his neighbors.

Although Papa Kweku maintained his fish store within the low-class district of Grassfield on the western side of the city and had a customer base of struggling buyers, he failed to cultivate any lasting friendship within this community.

As Papa Kweku made money and prosper, more and more of his fishing competitors began to harbor envy and jealousy for Papa Kweku. When reports surfaced that Papa Kweku had bribed a few tax collectors enabling him to escape paying his legitimate commercial taxes, government tax auditors pounced on the elderly businessman. Payment of high tax arreas and other penalties caused Papa Kweku business to collapse.

Under the cover of darkness, Papa Kweku nephew Tombux and a few loyal fishing crew members hopped into the largest of his Accra fishing canoes powered by a 75 HP Honda outboard motor and fled to his James town home in the heart of Accra. In less than three months after the crew arrived in James town, Papa Kweku suffered a massive heart attack and passed away.

As nephew Tombux sat with the grieving family listening to the funeral orator, he was struck by a particular admonition from the pulpit. The orator told the grieving audience that while many business people worked hard to develop a customer base, many of them forgot to establish enduring friendships in the communities in which they lived and operate their businesses.

Nephew Tombux did not take long to embark upon a new business strategy. His business maxim will be different from that of his late uncle Kweku. It would target both consumers as well as loyal and reliable friends.

Armed with this new consumer and friendship strategy, nephew Tombux and his fishing crew members boarded their fishing canoe and returned to Robertsport. After the customary 30 days grieving period ended, nephew Tombux rolled up his sleeves and went to work rebuilding the business he had inherited from his late uncle. The fishing business took off and prosperity returned. Tombux got married and had twins-a boy and a girl.

It was during a holiday visit with my high school classmate and friend Kwame who was one half of Tombux's twins that afforded Mr. Tombux the opportunity of sharing the rest of his life story with us.

The setting was at the breakfast table. There was a platter of boiled cassava, eddoes and sweet potatoes. There was also a steaming dish of well-seasoned red snapper, slices of barracuda, lobster, shrimp and other marine delicacies. The breakfast table was also adorned with freshly cut avocados, pineapple, oranges, and other fruits. Coffee, tea and other hot beverages were also served.

The wave from the ocean splashed ashore as we were enjoying our breakfast from a flower decked back porch. As high school student from all boys dominated catholic school, we were encouraged by our instructors to ask questions and show curiosity whenever we were privileged to be in the company of the parents of our friends as well as other external encounters.

It was Saturday morning and the rays of the sun danced on the surface of the Atlantic Ocean. Mr. Tombuck was in a relaxed mood after encouraging the high school friends of his son Kwame to enjoy their breakfast. He declared that he was going to share with us – mostly high school students – the secret of his business success. After narrating to the group, the reason why his uncle's business failed, he declared that his goal was to make friends within four targeted groups: the local government bureaucracy including the city major and chief of police, the educational bureaucracy including the superintendent and school principals, the local business community including the fishing sector and last but not the least the public.

Mr. Tombux observed that whenever he had issues regarding commercial licenses, tax payment and other regulatory matters, he knew exactly who to contact. When he needed to get a child or a relative into a school of his choice, he knew the person that had the leverage to get his aim accomplish. He further noted that he had befriended the movers and shakers not only in the fishing business but folks in the general business communities. Lastly, although Robertsport was an urban community, he was aware that the Vais were the dominant tribal group in Robertsport.

If a Vai male or female shopper did not have the full amount he charged for a bag of bunny fish, he would tell the shopper to take the product home. He will remind them to bring the balance amount when they came back to shop. He would call Vai male shoppers manja – the honorific name of choice – reminding them to bring back the amount owed during their next visit.

For a lady with a shopping list that included snapper, barracuda, shrimp and catfish – she is never turned away if her money is short. Calling such shoppers big mom, boss lady or for teenagers' fine girl your balance is this amount, you can bring it during your next shopping visit. Older business people in Robertsport will tell upcoming business people that the Vais are a proud bunch.

Honorific names usually disarm the buying public, most of those with cash balances usually close their account during their next visit. The bottom line for young people is quite simple, Mr. Tombux declare to our group. If you are selective in choosing your friends and take care to ensure that they will be there when the times are good or bad, you are most likely to succeed in your business and personal relationships.

As we broke up to get ready for the soccer, volley ball and other leisure activities on the sun-drenched beaches that afternoon, the lyric for my song, "We are buddies and trusted friends" began to dance before my very eyes. The advice from Mr. Tombux to our group made composing my song "We are buddies and trusted friends" an easy task. A full text of the song "we are buddies and trusted friends" can be found at the end of this story. Then next will be the English lyrics of the song "we are buddies and trusted friends".

We are buddies + Trusted friends

Buddies and friends

_We_ Need a country that meet our needs

And leaders with solutions

No matter the call, I be there with you

We are buddies and trusted friends

M U S I C

WE need friends to share our pain

Sharing the goods and bad times too

No matter the call I be there with you

We are buddies and trusted friends

M U S I C

WE need a place to share our dreams

Where   believers and others meet

No matter the call I be there with you

We are buddies and trusted friends

M U S I C

Let's unite in all we face

Whether tan, black or white

No matter the call I be there with you

WE are buddies and trusted friends

M U S I C

"Working People Rapping"

"Working People Rapping" is the third song in our contemporary and transitional song category. Once again, our Po-meh-nus and their cohorts provided the oral perspective regarding the mores precepts and value of this song. These values championed by our Po-meh-nus and their cohorts embellished the same value found in the cast of characters this composer was fortunate to work and interact with at various locations as diverse as the Goodrich plantation, its Monrovia office and offices in Midtown, Manhattan, USA. The Po-meh-nus and their cohorts encouraged this author to take note of the fact that the song "Working People Rapping" memorializes similar ingredients found in the popular Liberian parable – (monkey work baboo draw) – meaning some folks work while others relaxed, goof off and enjoy themselves.

The full message of working people rapping can only be understood when our readers share this composer's experiences with the characters he worked with and befriended over a span of 30 years.

There are two major groups of characters profiled by events surrounding this song. The first group of characters are the many Liberian workers – gola, vai, kpelle, bassa, lorma, gio, mano and other guest workers – employed by the Goodrich Rubber Plantation located on the eastern banks of the Lofa river. The composer's parents-Alpha-a labor relation officer and Sara, the company school teacher were part and parcel of the local work force.

They along with other local workers that lived in the community housing with names such as Mambo camp, Factory camp, Married camp as well as Clerk's quarters. None of these housing complexes had indoor toilet facilities. Recreational facilities were few and far apart. It is in these communities that the composer lived during the long summer school holidays.

The second group of characters were known as the expatriate staff. The expatriate staff had two sub groups – the local people named one sub group the siesta boys. These were expats drawn from cities such as Lisbon, Leon and Madrid. These expats worked mostly in the field. They supervised the local rubber planters, tappers and latex collectors. They ran the electric power plants, the maintenance garage and the rubber processing factory. They toiled alongside the local workers under the blazing sun and the torrential rain doing the company's business.

The second sub group were called the big boss men by the workers. These big boss men or expatriates hailed from cities such as Akron, the Florida Keys and Toronto. This group was represented by the general manager, chief financial officer, medical director and other senior officers.

Due to their cultural practices, the European expatriates work from 7am to 12 noon. Their lunch and siesta was between 12 noon and 3pm in the afternoon. Their work day ended at 6pm. The joke among the local workers was that by the time the European expatriates ended their work day at 6pm, took their dinner at 10pm and took to their bed just before midnight, they had no choice but to grab some lunch and have a long siesta between 12noon and 3pm the next day. In the meantime, the big boss men were known as people who could not wait to get off work at 4pm, grab an early snack and off to play their games of tennis and golf. This potential composer and other members of the local community were amused when their big boss men associates refer to the European expatriates as lazy employees only interested in having long siestas.

Friends like rubber planter Manuel and heavy-duty mechanic Antonio were gleeful as they pointed out big boss man Atkim and Ja-ro speeding in their Ford 150 pickup trucks to their beloved tennis and golf courts.

While Manuel and Antonio took this potential offer on fishing trips, it was big boss man Ja-ro who took him from the drudgery of rubber plantation work and placed him in-charge of the company's Monrovia office.

The Monrovia office job was relatively simple. The job entails taking purchase order to the stores of various vendors picking up the supplies, typing up a shipping list, loading the supplies on the company's vehicle and ensuring that the vehicle departed the Monrovia office precisely at 3pm to arrive at the plantation warehouse office no later than 4pm – Monday through Friday.

Out of college and basically working as a procurement clerk for a good part of 2 years, this aspiring manager was burnt out. A USAID notice in a local newspaper announcing the date for competitive exams for graduate study abroad was exactly what the doctor ordered for this enterprising graduate.

The graduate opportunity offered by the USAID scholarship, propelled my education at UNIFE (now Awolowo University). A British council sponsored fellowship at the Victoria University of Manchester followed. I was also a beneficiary of a GTZ sponsored fellowship at the PEPC in Berlin, Germany. My ensuing post graduate studies at Concordia

University in St. Paul, Minnesota coupled with my previous educational opportunities set me on a course for interesting jobs in the governmental bureaucracy.

More than 20 years had elapsed since I talked to folks like Ja-ro from my Goodrich plantation days. As I sat at my desk in my office at 5th and 45th street in Midtown, Manhattan, the phone rang at my secretary's desk. She answered the phone and inquired about the caller. She dialed my extension and informed me that there was a Ja-ro on the phone. I asked my secretary to pass Ja-ro unto me. I immediately recognized that husky sounding extroverted voice inquiring, is this AJK? He asked. As I replied is this Ja-ro? He responded with "what's up kiddo? Just as he behaved on the 2-way radio between the Monrovia and Goodrich offices some 20 years earlier. We exchanged pleasantries and inquired about each other's families.

He proceeded to inform me that he had a business opportunity in New York in 2 weeks and we agreed to meet for dinner. After sharing an early Friday evening dinner, Ja-ro told me that he hadn't had Liberian food since he departed Liberia and wish to have some of that good old cassava leaf dish. He indicated that he had nothing to do over the week-end. I proceeded to invite him to spend the week-end at my New Brunswick condo. We had the cassava leaf dish, fufu and soup and had a jolly good time over the week-end.

As he prepared to depart New York city on a Monday evening red eye flight, we sat at a corner table at the Algonquin hotel restaurant enjoying an evening dinner. We reminisce about our Goodrich plantation days. Ja-ro recalled the ongoing gossip that went on between his group, the North American bosses referred to as bamboo chillers and the European expatriates known among the Liberia workers as the monkey workers.

This monkey work, baboon draw gossips evoked a burst of good nature laughter between Ja-ro and I. our frolicking and laughing caused other restaurant patrons to keep stirring at us. They were probably wondering what was so amusing to those two gentlemen who appeared so different in their look and appearances. For Ja-ro and I, this was a welcoming opportunity to renew our friendship and we totally enjoyed each other's company.

The consensus shared by the Liberian group including the A.T. Sherman, Patrick and Rebecca Johnson, P.S. Freeman, Barclay's, Grants, Scotts, Coleman, Sambolas, Johnny Johnson, Oretha, Joe Mason, Manuel and Antonio of the Siesta as well as the golfing group used the monkey work bamboo draw phrase as a sarcastic joke commonly shared among friends. The sarcasm was not intended to belittle individuals or groups, neither were the jokes intended to besmirch anyone's character or reputation.

Everyone in all three of the groups along with this author's monkey working and bamboo chilling song, sees no contradiction between working and toiling all day long and taking off time to relax, chill and have a jolly good time in the evening hours.

As we departed the Algonquin, Ja-ro hopped in the back seat of his taxi cab, headed for the airport and we have not seen each other since that memorable dinner party.

During the intervening years I ended up on the wrong side of the political spectrum. Following the Liberian civil war, I ended up losing my job and my pension benefit. Stressed and traumatized, I was attacked by an aggressive form of glaucoma leading to total blindness in both eyes. Diabetic and impacted with other blood ailments, I would have ended it all in the manner of past Shakespearian tragedies.

After some deep introspection and reflections, I gather my experiences during the Goodrich Plantation days to compose my song – "Working People Rapping" with the recurrent chorus – yes to monkey working – no to bamboo chilling – which can be found at the end of this story. Next will be the English lyrics for the song "Working People Rapping".

"Working People Rapping"

1. Dozers are moving
   Bushes are clearing
   Rubber trees are growing
   It's working people rapping

2. Rubber trees are growing
   Rubber farm is bigger
   It's all maturing
   It's working people rapping

3. Tappers are cutting
   Latex is flowing
   Rubber products are coming
   It's working people rapping

4. All shifts are closing
   All workers are feasting
   No monkey working – no baboon golfing
   It's working people rapping

5. Are working people rapping?
   Yes, they are rapping
   See working people working?
   It's working people rapping

6. Are working people rapping?
   Yes, they are rapping
   See working people working
   It's working people rapping

"Happy Birthday"

Our oral story telling Po-meh-nus and their cohorts had their own concept about how birthdays are celebrated. They appeared receptive to birthday celebration practices from different cultures. They agreed that different societies celebrate birth anniversaries according to their cultural norms, mores, folkways, values and unique traditions. The most cherished celebration in the rural community of which this author hailed centers around food. The birthday celebrant is usually given a big bowl of rice topped with a sauce they yearned for. The daily sauce may contain chicken wings and feet. On the celebrant's natal day things take a dramatic turn. The rice bowl does not only have the chicken wing and feet. The celebrant is also given chicken thigh along with the chicken breast and neck. Over the years, the birthday food has evolved in many cultures with a variety of dishes, pastries, special cakes and beverages

Many cultures have expanded their gifts to include Harley Davidson bikes, cash, fiber glass Honda powered pleasure boats, gold and diamond rings, Rolex watches, Dolce & Gabbana fragrances, trips on carnival cruise line and a variety of other gifts.

Sometimes during the 20th century two sisters named Pat and Mildred Hill from Louisville, Kentucky decided to add a new dimension to the tapestry of birthday gift giving. As the elder sister Mildred's birthday approached, the younger sister Pat sat down and wrote some uplifting lyrics to commemorate her sister's birthday. Older sister Mildred – a trained musician read the lyrics and decided to set a musical tune to her sister Pat's memorable words.

Pat's lyrics and Mildred's tune have produced what is commonly called the happy birthday song. The happy birthday song for many generations have serenaded kings, queens, princes, princesses and more than half a billion ordinary folks across the globe.

Other versions of the happy birthday song composed by Prince Niko, including this composer should not have been possible without the trail blazing musical contribution of the Hill sisters of Louisville, Kentucky.

My version of the happy birthday song celebrates the lives of all manner of people born and yet unborn. They are challenged to perform extraordinary tasks – no matter what they do and how they do it. Families and friends must always ask themselves to jump and rejoice as they celebrate their birthday anniversaries. Our version of the Hill sister's happy birthday song can be found at the end of this story. Next will be the English lyrics of the song "Happy Birthday".

"Happy Birthday"

1. Happy Birthday to you
   Happy Birthday to you
   Happy Birthday to you dear
   Happy Birthday to you

2. How old are you
   How young are you
   No matter your age dear pal
   Happy Birthday to you

3. How tall are you
   How short are you
   No matter your height dear pal
   Happy Birthday to you

4. How rich are you
   How poor are you
   No matter your purse dear pal
   Happy Birthday to you

5. We wish you success
   We wish you good health
   Ain't matter your health dear pal
   Happy Birthday to you

6. Happy Birthday dear pal
   We wish you success
   We wish you good health
   Happy Birthday to our pal
   Happy Birthday to you

EPILOGUE

Our book singing and dancing across Liberia profiles 15 indigenous Liberian songs broken down into a part "A" and "B" sections of the book. The seven (7) part "A" songs are phonetically written and originate from the Vai dialect. They emanate out of the folkways, mores and traditional values of Vai culture. The singers and musicians of these songs are simple folks whose songs entertain themselves and their immediate families. The songs convey messages of pain, anguish, disappointments and occasional joyous moments. These songs normally celebrate the planting of rice – the staple diet of the rice farmers and their families. The songs also lionize the lives of a selected number of local personalities. Some of these personalities live heroic lives while the lives of others leave much to be desired. Many of the songs celebrate extraordinary events which impact the lives of the rural dwellers. Other songs describe the beauty as well as the squalor of the environment circumstances forced them to live in.

The oral narratives regarding the development and evolution of these value laden folksy and traditional songs were given voice by the Wo-meh-nus, Mem-meh-ku-meh-nus and Po-meh-nus who are normally regarded as the spokes people and guardians of their communities. Having profiled the seven (7) part "A" songs the Wo-meh-nus and their cohorts gently steer this author towards an examination of the part "B" songs. The background of these songs and perspective about the stories regarding their origins can be mind bugging. Some of the stories narrated by our Mem-meh ku-meh-nus and their cohorts explores the lives of both cultural giants as well as sneaky dwarfs. Some of these lives and events evoke stories that are nostalgic as well as hilarious and satirical. What remains irrefutable is the fact that the story concerns the lives of both rural and urban dwellers struggling to be heard as they grapple with their activities of daily living. As this author listened to oral narrations of both the cunning and lofty legends and stories painstakingly laid out during lengthy sessions with our local spokes people a few long-term goals began to emerge for the author. First, this author decided that the life stories that the singers and musicians lionized in their songs and shared by the local spokes people should be publicize. Second, the author would strive to put the rambling oral narratives into standardize lyrics. Third, the standardize lyrics would be set to melodious tones easily recognized by members of the rural and urban communities. The fourth goal would be the publication of a book containing the professional profiling of all 15 songs.

It is the expectation of this author that this book of genuine and authentic Liberian songs shall serve as a primary source material for the general as well as serve as an instructional tool by music teachers of young Liberians enroll in institutions of learning scattered across Liberia. An additional dream of this author is that music lovers in diverse communities such as Clay Ashland and Cebu city, Bomoja and Birmingham and the depressed areas of West Point and Washington DC can assemble their dancing partners on dance floors and boogie-weegie to the melodious sounds of the fifteen (15) songs profiled in this book. This author is further convinced that if he with all his physical and medical challenges can compose, rearrange and have his 15 songs publish anyone else in similar circumstances can accomplish the same dreams. We are therefore excited to welcome our Liberian and global musical audience on this unique musical adventure.

REFERENCE NOTES

The project undertaken by this author to profile (15) songs in our book titled "Singing and Dancing Across Liberia" could not have been possible without the collaborative assistance of the Wo-meh-nus, Man-meh-ku-meh-nus, Po-meh-nus and their cohorts. The (3) groups embodied the totality of information, knowledge, experience and insightful perspective on the folkways, mores, traditions and values of their rural as well as the urban environment in which they live. Their oral narratives concerning an array of personalities, momentous events and geographic locations is simply astonishing. Although the Wo-meh-nus and their cohorts prefer anonymity, this author feels duty bound to provide recognition to a selected few for going above and beyond the call of civic responsibilities. We fondly recall the services of the Suamanna, Marbu, Siafa Luma, Momo Kondo, Jebeh Adji, Sambolas, Paasewes, Burphy, Zuanna Sherman, Simpsons, Wrights, Dakehs, McGills, Gbessey Freeman, Gottohs, Darblahs, Kamaras, Kromahs, Worgbehs, Fahnhos, Kandakais, Kemokais, Kiadiis, Fahnbullehs, Bai Dodohs, Bai T. Moores, Bakanas, Tombaykai Dempster, Wiles, Grimes, Massaquois, Charlie B. Sherman, Tuan Wreh, Jangaba Johnson and many others.

The scions of these illustrious personalities embodied our Wo-meh-nus, Men-meh-ku-meh-nus, Po-meh-nus and their cohorts. During their lengthy interactions with this author our oral narrators decided to focus their attention on (4) specific category of individuals and subject matters: Various singers and musicians, an array of iconic personalities, momentous events and prescribed geographic locations.

The oral narrators cited singers who sang folksy music to sooth their pains, anguish and disappointments. They were mostly singer farmers with no education. They hummed and sang songs with limited lyrics to entertain themselves and family members. Others performed for larger gatherings following the rice harvest and the many feasts and festivals that the young and old could not wait to take part in.

The bibliographysical citations now follows:

> Marinelli's book "The New Liberia" corroborates the importance the Vais attached to the planting of their staple food product – Rice – in the lives of rural dwellers. The bibliographical citation follows: The New Liberia by Lawrence A. Marinelli, published for the African Service Institute of New York by Frederick A. Praeger, New York, London, 1964, p14.

> Additional affirmation of Vai farming practices also found in "The Land of the Pepper Bird" by Sidney De La Rue, New York, London, The Knickerbocker Press 1930, p276.

> De La Rue's "Land of the Pepper Bird" also glorifies the importance music and dance place in the lives of typical villagers after retiring home from their farms and other mundane daily task. The bibliographical citation follows: "Land of the Pepper Bird" by Sidney De La Rue, New York, London, The Knickerbocker Press, 1930 p181.

> The synchronizing rice cleaning procedure is also corroborated in De La Rue's book "The Land of the Pepper Bird. Bibliographical citation follows: The Land of the Pepper Bird, by Sidney De La Rue, New York, London, The Knickerbockers Press, 1930, p277.

> The Land of the Pepper Bird" by author De La Rue illuminates the wisdom of the gray beards. The bibliographical citation follows: "The Land of the Pepper Bird" by Sidney De La Rue, New York, London, The Knickerbocker Press, 1903, p91, p92, p93, & p94.

> This sentiment is corroborated in Daily Observer's Keith N.A. Best's book "The Other Side of Roots". The bibliographical citation follows: The Other Side of Roots" by Keith Neville Asumuyaya Best, copyright © 1994, all Rights Reserved, (404) 956.0979, p31

> The criticism of the inaptitude by the Liberian political classes to manage the country's fiscal resources is corroborated in S. Augustu P. Horton's book "Liberia's Underdevelopment-In Spite of The

Struggle". Copyrighted in 1994 by University Press of America, Inc Lanhan, Maryland. See citation on p26, p27.

➤ Many personalities-some iconic and others villainous – caught the attention of our esteem oral narrators. The Dwalu Bukelleh Vai invention story is a stark illustration of an iconic personality. This oral narrator is corroborated by "The New Liberia" by Lawrence A. Marinelli, published by the African Service Institute of New York by Frederick A. Praeger, publishers, New York, London, 1964, p13.

➤ The boy Leopard encounter with the village chief and his elders regarding the chicken breast and chicken neck episode reminds us of a villainous personality. This story is corroborated by an account in "The Land of the Pepper Bird" by Sidney De La Rue, New York, London, The Knickerbocker Press, 1903, pages 91, 92, 93, & 94.

➤ The Wo-men-nus, Mem-meh-ku-meh-nus and Po-meh-nus were quick in pointing out to this author that the visitation of the sooth sailing family to the Yardi village, its chief and gullible villagers vividly illustrates the significance of a momentous encounter between two groups with diametrically opposing philosophies.

➤ Ever respectful of their Kru compatriots the Wo-meh-nus, Mem-meh-ku-men-nus and Po-meh-nus solemnly asserted in heated debate before this author that the Sasstown conflict was an important example to all Liberians on the need to defend one's birth right even if the outcome of the conflict has little or no chance of success. What was even more important was how quickly one accepted the reality of defeat and quickly proceeded to embrace one's Liberian identity.

➤ The Wo-meh-nus and their cohorts' perspective of the Krus unique personality on the Liberian scene is corroborated by their strategic location of a sizable chunk on the western cost of Liberia. This bibliographical citation can be found in "The New Liberia" by Lawrence A. Marinelli, published by the Africa Service Institute of New York by Frederick A. Praeger, New York, London, pages19, 20.

The Wo-meh-nus, Mem-meh-ku-meh-nus, Po-men-nus and their cohorts were of the consensus that the sande and porro bush schools provided the venue where the singers, musicians, musical instrumental players, dancers and performers obtained their rudimentary musical skills and other artistic endowments. They also unanimously agreed that there were significant musical influences from the So-so and the Fulani tribes of the sahel region. They also took note of the impact of the ju-ju music from Uroba land and other communities of the Delta region. The highlife musical genre emanating from communities across Accra, Tema and Seconde are noteworthy. The masanta beat from the Guinean highland coupled with the patois assented songs and music with that creo rhythm from our neighboring Shebro and Gallianas neighbors have all helped to enrich our Liberian musical tapestry. Notwithstanding these influences the irrefutable fact remains that the (15) songs profiled in this book are authentically Liberian. We will be remiss in our duties if we did not report to our musical audience the serious shortage of books containing authentic Liberian music. It is our fervent hope that singing and dancing across Liberia will serve as a teaching tool for music instructors serving in institutions of learning across Liberia.

Acknowledgement

This author owes a debt of gratitude to our Wo-meh-nus, Men-men-ku-meh-nus and Po-meh-nus for the oral narratives and perspective they generously shared with this author during several decades of work on this publication. We are also grateful for the corroborative information obtained from several publications utilized by us in our reference notes and bibliographical citations. I am also grateful to USAID, The British Council and the GTZ for the funding provided me to pursue my graduate studies. Deep gratitude is extended to my scribes Anthony K. Hammond and Christine Johnson for helping me with this project. Others I am indebted to are granddaughters – Moriah Johnson-my illustrator and Amaya Johnson-my formatting assistant. My deepest gratitude goes to my parents Alpha, Sarah and grandfather Zukeh Kandakai of Jundu. My love and affection goes to my wife Victoria, my children, grandchildren and the rest of my family. I am also grateful to my publishers and others who have help me with this project. All errors and omissions are mine and mine only. ....

Printed in the United States
By Bookmasters